SPLENDOR OF THE SAINTS

SPLENDOR OF THE SAINTS

HOW THEY DAZZLE THE WORLD AND SHAPE HISTORY

FR. ALOYSIUS ROCHE

TAN Books
Charlotte, North Carolina

Nihil Obstat:
Georgius Can. Smith, S.Th.D., Ph.D.
Censor deputatus

Imprimatur:
✠ Joseph Butt, *Vic. Gen.*
Westmonasterii,
die 14th Januarii 1936

This book was first published in 1936 by London, Burns, Oates & Washbourne, Ltd., in London. The TAN Edition has been re-typeset and revised to include corrections of typographical and occasional factual errors; updated style, vocabulary, punctuation, and spelling; Scripture citations; and new bibliographic and explanatory footnotes.

Cover image: *The Landauer Altarpiece, All Saints Day,* 1511 (oil on panel), Dürer, Albrecht (1471–1528) / Kunsthistorisches Museum, Vienna, Austria / Bridgeman Images

ISBN: 978-1-61890-607-6

Cataloging-in-Publication data on file with the Library of Congress

Printed and bound in the United States of America

TAN Books
Charlotte, North Carolina
www.TANBooks.com

2016

"Ah, but a man's reach should exceed his grasp,
Or what's a heaven for?"

Robert Browning, "Andrea del Sarto"

CONTENTS

FOREWORD

FATHER Aloysius Roche, said one of his contemporaries, "has the gift of making saints fascinating." In *Splendor of the Saints,* first published in London in 1936, he displays that gift in abundance, with a cheerful, even childlike charm. His view of the saints reflects a sense of wonder and delight that is at once refreshing and contagious.

Perhaps Fr. Roche's winsome attitude toward our elder brothers and sisters in the Faith sprang from his own childhood experience. He had plenty of siblings to look up to: Born in Dundee, Scotland, in 1886 to a Welsh convert mother and an Irish Catholic father, he was one of sixteen children and the youngest of ten sons. Remarkably, four of the boys were to become priests.

The family owned a grocery store in town where young Aloysius worked for several years after high school. When at last he discerned a priestly vocation, he was accepted into the Redemptorist novitiate at Bishop Eton in Liverpool in 1904 and was professed in 1908. He completed his seminary training in 1914 at St. Mary's Monastery in Kinnoul, Perth, Scotland, and was ordained that year by Bishop Robert Fraser.

Fr. Roche began his ministry in Liverpool, and from

there he launched his first parish mission work. But by 1917, health problems led him to affiliate with the Diocese of Brentwood as a secular priest. After several months at Walthamstow, he was assigned to the town of Billericay in 1918. There he remained as parish priest for forty-eight years.

PEN AND PULPIT

As director of the Brentwood Diocesan Catholic Evidence Guild, Fr. Roche became widely known as a Catholic apologist through his preaching and writing. He spoke frequently on the BBC Silver Lining program and later made television appearances as well. He was especially popular as a preacher in the London area.

Those sermons and lectures provided the substance for many of the twenty-eight books he published. Despite his busy schedule as a pastor and preacher, between 1932 and 1955 Fr. Roche averaged nearly one book a year, publishing three titles in 1938 alone.

Reflecting his childlike spirit, his "first excursion into the field of literature," as he put it, was entitled *Talks for Girls* (1932). It was the fruit of numerous retreats he had preached for children. Other titles for children and youth followed, such as *Talks for Young Women* (1938); *The Boyhood of a Priest* (1938); *A Night of Adventure; or, The Four Musketeers* (1940); *All Aboard the Centurion* (1945); *Animals Under the Rainbow* (1950); and *Christians Courageous: Tales of Christian Adventure* (1955). Asked once about his favorites among the numerous books he had published, he admitted: "My own partiality is for works addressed to young readers."

Meanwhile, Fr. Roche's adult audiences had their favorites among his titles as well—celebrated works such as *A Bedside Book of Saints* (1934), for which *Splendor of the Saints* (1936) was an equally popular companion work; *Apologetics for the Pulpit* (3 volumes, 1935–1936); *The Things That Matter* (1941); *Knots and Crosses* (1942); and *Mystery Man, or The Catholic Priest Explained* (1950). He once noted with characteristic humility: "My best work is undoubtedly the one I hope to write someday."

Fr. Roche maintained his energetic ministry of pen and pulpit for more than half a century. He did not retire until 1966, at the age of eighty. He died two years later, still young at heart.[1]

SAINTS THAT DAZZLE

Countless books about the saints have been written. What distinctive angle of vision does this one present to make it worthy of a new edition for a new generation?

According to the author's preface, his earlier work, *The Bedside Book of Saints,* laid the stress "upon those qualities which it is customary to speak of as human. One and all the saints were human, and it is always useful to remind ourselves of the fact." But that human aspect was

---

1 Bernard Aspinwall and Stewart Foster, "The Second Apostolates of Two Scottish Priests in Inter-War Essex: Reverend John Charleson (1862–1942) and Rev. Aloysius Roche (1886–1868)," *The Innes Review* 54, no. 1 (Spring 2003): 109–110; Matthew Hoehn, O.S.B., ed., *Catholic Authors: Contemporary Biographical Sketches* (Morristown, N.J.: St. Mary's Abbey, 1952), 485–486. I am grateful to Colby Hunter of the Chestatee Regional Library System, Dawsonville, Georgia, for his invaluable assistance in research for the author's biography. His diligent work has helped me more than once.

only half their story, and "it would not do to strike the human note in the saints too emphatically or to pause over it for too long. This might easily reconcile us to our own mediocrity."[2]

For this reason, the present work soon followed that book to complete the picture. "We all chafe against the monotony of the humdrum and commonplace, and we reach out to the exceptional and the heroic," Fr. Roche observed. "It is this scaling of the heights, this ecstasy of soul, these elements of the exceptional and the heroic, that constitute *Splendor of the Saints*."[3]

Even so, the author resists the temptation to which many writers have succumbed: He does not focus primarily on the miracles of the saints. His eye may be on the exceptional, but it is not on the sensational. Though he may examine here what he calls the "dazzling" aspects of their lives, it is not the glitter of preternatural fireworks. Rather, he marvels at the brilliance of valiant deeds and heroic dimensions, the extraordinary saintly features that serve to stir us, to hold our attention, to inspire us to follow them, and ultimately to sanctify us.

With each characteristic examined, Fr. Roche paints these saintly portraits against the background of secular celebrities from history. In this way, he shows by contrast not only how much more brightly the saints shine, but also how much more worthy they are of our attention and imitation.

Do our hearts thrill to read the romantic adventures

2 See Preface, xix.

3 Preface, xxi.

of the past? The romance of the saints is more thrilling, and more honorable, still: "The knights fought with robbers and tyrants and giants. The saints fought with the Devil, the world, and the flesh. Both knights and saints leave home and country: the first in search of adventure, the second in quest of penance and peace."[4]

The recollections of the British explorer Captain James Cook are certainly teeming with romantic adventure. But in those pages "we shall find nothing so exciting as the story of St. Francis Xavier's voyage to the Indies.... Daniel Defoe's immortal *Robinson Crusoe* is largely a work of imagination. But what romantic tales could be written round the authentic facts of the lives of the ancient solitaries and hermits."[5]

And what of the powerful, influential movers and shakers who are lionized by secular historians? "The power exemplified in the pages of history," Fr. Roche observes, "is mainly the power of brute force, and its idols, when closely inspected, turn out to have feet of clay—and commonly very dirty clay at that."[6]

On the other hand, he notes, "against the depressing background of secular history, there stands out serene and consoling the contribution to history which we call the lives of the saints. They present to us the most encouraging of all spectacles: that of heroes and conquerors victorious in the service of a really good cause."[7] Where now are the glories of the arrogant, ruthless Nero? Yet the global

4 Chapter 2, "A Wonderful World of Romance," 12.

5 "Romance," 14–15.

6 Chapter 3, "The Saints in History," 28.

7 "History," 30.

and gracious impact of St. Francis of Assisi remains.

And so it goes, as the author illustrates each saintly characteristic with abundant examples. Again and again, the saints far outshine the children of the world in unselfish sacrifice and relentless self-denial; in boundless energy and extravagant generosity; in pioneering enlightenment and undying legacy; in the accomplishments of heroic deeds and the endurance of unspeakable sufferings.

VEGETARIANISM AND ANIMAL RIGHTS

Splendor of the Saints no doubt has its debatable points. Certain occasional remarks about women, for example, sound dismissive or patronizing to those of our time, though they probably express common sentiments of the author's generation.

The book also reflects at times what will seem to some readers as the author's idiosyncrasies. Others, of course, might consider the same concerns to be pioneering.

Fr. Roche was sympathetic, for example, to the "food reform" movement of his time, which sought "to end the enormous scandal of the modern diet." Given the widespread concern for healthier eating in our day—if not a comparable reform in actual eating habits—Fr. Roche seems to speak prophetically when he notes that "the day is approaching when in the interests of the higher spirituality the whole question of diet will have to be reexamined."[8] In his chapter on "The Diet of the Saints," he goes so far as to enlist their example as support for

8 Chapter X, "The Diet of the Saints," 144, 147.

vegetarianism.

In another chapter, "The Enlightenment of the Saints," Fr. Roche notes how saints were often ahead of their time with regard to other social movements of "reformation and improvement." The passage in that chapter on saints and animals objects vehemently, not only to commonly recognized forms of animal cruelty, but also to "blood sports"—that is, hunting. On this point he is in fact able to cite the condemnation of hunting as a "hellish pleasure" by St. Francis de Sales.[9]

The depth of the author's feelings on this matter are indicated by the passion of his language:

> This "average good Christian" of the twentieth century has been told so often that the animals have "no rights." He has been warned so often that he must be very, very, very careful not to get sentimental about them. So he has come to believe that this emphatic "No Rights!" and this emphatic "No Sentiment!" have settled the matter between them.
>
> "*Causa finita est*—the case is closed! So let's get on with our hunting and our trapping and our vivisecting and our maiming and laming and big game shooting. Animals can have no rights, so evidently they can suffer no wrongs. How very sensible our religion is!"[10]

9 Chapter X, "The Enlightenment of the Saints, 131.

10 "Enlightenment," 128–29.

Fr. Roche's words in this chapter and in his book *These Animals of Ours* (1939)[11] have in fact been cited repeatedly by "animal rights" advocates of our day.

It was in defense of this cause that Fr. Roche offered two extended quotes that he thought to have come from saintly sources. One he presented as an observation about St. Francis of Assisi by St. Bonaventure. The other he cited as words from the ancient Liturgy of St. Basil.[12]

In fact, however, the first can nowhere be found in Bonaventure's biography of Francis, though there are a few phrases in that text which might have been borrowed and expanded by a later writer. Meanwhile, the words attributed to the Liturgy of St. Basil actually come from an American Baptist leader in the "Social Gospel" movement of the early twentieth century.[13] To those familiar with ancient and medieval texts, as Fr. Roche no doubt was, the modern-sounding language of both quotes should have aroused suspicions. Perhaps the intensity of his feelings explains why he was not as careful as he might have been to verify their sources.

All in all, however, *Splendor of the Saints* provides a convincing case for the high heroism of holiness, in all its remarkable achievements and captivating beauty. Fr. Roche offers manifold evidence for the exceptional qualities of saintly life, which radiate a magnetism that attracts us, a light that leads us, and a power that transforms us.

---

11 *These Animals of Ours* (London: Burns, Oates, Washbourne, 1939).

12 "Enlightenment," 129–31.

13 See note 105.

NOTES ON THE TAN EDITION

A few notes are in order about this TAN edition of the book, which involved much more than a simple reprinting or even re-typesetting. First, the text has been slightly revised to update vocabulary, punctuation, style, and format. These revisions should make the work more accessible to a twenty-first-century audience.

Second, biblical quotations now have citations within the text. The author used the Douay-Rheims version of the Bible, and that version has been retained.

Third, the book now has footnotes. When it was first published in 1936, editorial standards for citing sources, even of direct quotations, were not nearly as rigorous in popular works as they are today. Fr. Roche was especially fond of quoting, but he often failed to provide the title of the quotation's source text and, in many cases, even the name of the author. Occasional errors appeared in the quotations themselves. The abundant Internet resources now available allowed for the correction of errors and the identification of most (but not all) of the relevant sources. The result is more than a hundred new notes.

Finally, because the author could assume a certain level of erudition in much of his audience, he often cited writers (especially historians) by surname only and without identification. To do otherwise might have insulted his readers, to whom these figures were usually well known. Many of these same writers, however, are largely unknown to today's readers. So first names and other identifying information have been added to the text itself where needed.

We take delight in making this book, with all its childlike wisdom and fascination, more available to readers today, updated and enhanced, and well deserving of a wide audience. The sketches of sanctity in these pages can help you on your own way to sainthood, as Fr. Roche reminds us: "If good company on the road is the best shortcut, we shall journey to heaven with all the less fatigue if God's saints are our travelling companions."[14]

Paul Thigpen, Ph.D.
Editor, TAN Books
November 1, 2015
Feast of All Saints

14 Chapter 1, "The Company of the Saints," 1.

PREFACE

IN an earlier book I wrote on the saints,[15] the stress was laid upon those qualities which it is customary to speak of as human. One and all the saints were human, and it is always useful to remind ourselves of the fact. But a human being is a composite production, with a quality that we may compare to a two-piece garment. When this human being develops as God intended, the result is a completion that is called *sanctity.*

In Holy Scripture the saint is likened to a tree planted by the running waters (see Ps 1:3)—planted, that is to say, in the open air where sun and wind can get at its leaves and where all its branches have room to expand. There is nothing stunted or one-sided about such a tree. It is literally an *all-round* success. And certainly there is nothing one-sided about holiness.

Besides, it would not do to strike the human note in the saints too emphatically or to pause over it for too long. This might easily reconcile us to our own mediocrity; and acquiescence in a mediocrity of Christian service is a very disturbing feature of our day. It is altogether

---

15 Aloysius Roche, *A Bedside Book of Saints* (repr., Long Prairie, Minn.: Neumann Press, 2001).

unfortunate that, as many have said, the "ordinary" man should be "the man of the hour," because this "ordinary" man insists upon dragging everything down to his own ordinary level.

If he is a Christian, then he swallows his Christianity in diluted and sweetened doses. To such, St. Francis is no more than the familiar and useful saint who forgives everyone and everything; the saint who talks with birds and shakes hands with wolves; the saint who does not lose himself in dogma but prefers to write poetry. These modern devotees have transformed the sorrowful figure of the Portiuncula Penitent into the image of a combed and smiling little saint with a pigeon on his shoulder.

In reality, there is nothing in the lives of the saints calculated to soothe this "ordinary" Christian. But then, as the Irish biographer of saints Alice Curtayne remarks, the purpose of such lives is not to soothe but to stir humanity. True, the saints were fashioned out of common clay. But their common clay, like ours, was vivified by the divine Breath, and it was animated by the divine spark called grace. Cooperation with this grace lifted them clean out of the common rut.

Here lies their real value and attraction. The extraordinary, the superlative, the unique is really what holds us and, above all, what regenerates us. The dazzling man, the dazzling woman, are objects of fascination.

The outstanding—a supremacy of virtue or sacrifice: before this, we are willing to kneel, and by this, we are prepared to be influenced. We all want to live in the sublime which, after all, is our true dwelling place—to quit the tiresome valley in which as exiles we are condemned to wander, to scale the heights and to get our heads among the stars. Even the least aspiring among us does covet a little ecstasy of soul.

In short, we all chafe against the monotony of the humdrum and commonplace, and we reach out to the exceptional and the heroic. It is this scaling of the heights, this ecstasy of soul, these elements of the exceptional and the heroic, that constitute the splendor of the saints.

In conformity with the decree of Pope Urban VIII, dated March 17, 1625, we declare that, if in the course of this work, we should give the name of saint to those not officially recognized as such; and if we make mention of such facts and revelations as might bear the character of the miraculous or prophetic; we do not in any way presume to take upon ourselves to express, on either persons or facts, a judgment which is reserved to the Church, nor in any way whatsoever to forecast decisions which belong to her alone.

THE COMPANY OF THE SAINTS

"IT is not good that the man should be alone" (Gn 2:18). This was one of the first remarks that God made about His human creatures. St. Alphonsus Liguori used to pray to be protected from himself, because he knew the peril that lurks in self-will and isolation. Whenever we go alone we go astray, for the little light that is in us serves to dazzle rather than to guide us.

If good company on the road is the best shortcut, we shall journey to heaven with all the less fatigue if God's saints are our travelling companions. And indeed they have walked by our side often enough if we only knew it. They have drawn near to us again and again, not in bodily presence, but in the guise of the inspirations and generous thoughts they have poured into our souls.

No mystery is more mysterious than the mystery of my own preservation. How have I contrived to keep afloat when so many who were made of stouter timber than I have foundered? Perhaps some saint famed while on earth for his strength and energy steadied the tottering ark of my existence by his prayer.

Down to date I have kept the faith, and this is no mean

achievement, as the boast of St. Paul surely implies (see 2 Tm 4:7). Perhaps the Apostle of the Gentiles himself has helped me to keep this treasure intact. Again and again I have emerged—scorched indeed, but yet breathing and living—from the fire of temptation. And it may be that some one or other of the Holy Innocents interceded for me by the memory of his sorrowful and unmerited martyrdom (see Mt 2:16–18).

Not once but many times I have strayed into a strange and forbidden territory like the Prodigal Son, and like him have eaten unworthy and deadly food (see Lk 15:11–32). If, like him, I have returned to my Father's home, it may have been that the impulse that drove me homewards came to me through one of those illustrious converts who climbed to heaven by the ladder of contrition and repentance. So many dangers avoided, so many calamities averted, so much misfortune turned aside, thanks to the intercession of those whose foreheads are signed with the sign of the living God, and out of respect for whom the angel of the Apocalypse said: "Do not harm the earth, or the sea, or the trees!" (Rv 7:3).

THE EXAMPLE OF THE SAINTS

Surely the virtues that dignify and ennoble our nature, and render human existence here below bearable and worthwhile, owe their vindication and preservation, under God, to the example of the saints. And the echo of that example has never been allowed to die away! For that kind of vindication and support, virtue has seldom been able to look to the so-called great men of the world.

After losing the battle for Rome, the Roman senator

Brutus (one of the assassins of Julius Caesar) fell upon his sword, saying that he had pursued virtue thinking it a substance, but he had found it to be only a shadow. "We shall accomplish but little in the world," said an eminent statesman, "and certainly we shall never govern successfully, if we rely only on the Ten Commandments and the Sermon on the Mount."

"Preachers," a modern philosopher writes, "may sound the praises of goodness; but serious philosophy, dissenting from the rabble, must believe that virtue has only been shown to man, has only been made attractive to man, in order, like the fruit of Tantalus, to sharpen his appetite and to madden him by the fact that it is beyond his reach."

But the saints have demonstrated by the splendor of their lives that virtue lies within the grasp of human hands, provided that these human hands are fortified by that grace that is offered to all. In one of his sermons, Venerable Bede enumerates these virtues. He speaks of chastity, humility, charity, and so on; and then he says: "These are the footprints that the saints on ascending to heaven left behind upon our earth, in order that we, following after, might attain to the same reward."

Someone wrote of the saints that they preserve the memory of forgotten things. Which of us ever thinks of praying to the Holy Innocents? Yet St. Francis de Sales often did. But the saints also preserve the memory of many a little virtue that otherwise might fall into neglect and decay.

Simplicity, for example, seems in these latter days to have been condemned to wander forlorn through a world that has no desire to entertain or to harbor it. Few are those who will give it a shelter and a home, and fewer still are those who are willing to wed it as St. Francis wed the Lady Poverty. Our piety has become so practical that we dismiss simplicity as being a virtue that will not work—or, if we are of a commercial turn of mind, as a virtue that does not pay.

"Let us die in our simplicity," said the saintly French archbishop François Fénelon—*"Moriamur in simplicitate nostra."* But sometimes one is tempted to think that Simplicity herself decided to die with Fenelon. Badly do we need this lesson, and the saints one and all can teach it to us. "The lives of the saints," historian J. A. Froude had to admit, "are always simple."[16]

THE CONSOLATION OF THE SAINTS

Live in the company of the saints, and you will never despair of your fellowman. A man's opinion of his species does depend to a great extent on the kind of company he keeps.

Public men are said to have rather a poor opinion of men, no doubt because public men are the only sort of men the public man knows. The Big Business man is fond of saying that honesty does not exist in this world, simply because he has never come across it in that very prominent but small part of the world represented by Big Business. And indeed this world-weary pessimism is a temptation that sooner or later assails most of us.

16 James Anthony Froude, "The Lives of the Saints," in *Short Studies on Great Subjects* (London: Longmans, Green, 1867), II, 203.

Our opinion of our fellowmen is apt to fall lower and lower the longer we live among them. "The more I know of men, the better I like my dog," the French people say, and there are many who quite agree with them. "The longer I live," concluded the German writer Johann Wolfgang von Goethe, "the more justified I feel in having a profound contempt for my fellow creatures."

It has been written of Giacomo Leopardi, the Italian poet of pessimism and despair who destroyed himself at the age of thirty-nine, that he became "one of those who know men and therefore despise them, a member of that company of spirits contemptuous of the world, to which in France Chamfort and La Bruyere belonged; in England, Byron and Oscar Wilde; and in Germany, Schopenhauer." Terrible cries of resentment and agony rose from the tortured heart of this man who could see good neither in himself nor in others:

> Now shalt thou rest for ever,
> Thou weary heart.
> Long enough hast thou beaten;
> Nought lives that were worth
> Thy throbbings, and the earth
> Merits no sigh. Bitter tedium
> Is our being, and the world, filth—nought else.
> Be still.

Mankind does, alas, sometimes appear to be rather a sordid assemblage of selfish, cruel beings superior to the brutes only in that they have more cleverness and cunning. But in the midst of this distressing mediocrity, glorious and numerous exceptions appear. "Were it not for the saints," says a modern writer, "I might despair of my fellow man."

John Henry Cardinal Newman, in his *Apologia,* speaks in vivid language of the depressing effect produced by this superficial view of human life and history. "To consider the world in its length and breadth . . . the many races of man . . . their mutual alienation, their conflicts . . the greatness and littleness of man . . . the defeat of good, the success of evil . . . the prevalence . . . of sin . . . all this is a vision to dizzy and appall."[17]

But intercourse with the saints means that imperceptibly our ideals are not only raised a little higher but are confirmed and corroborated, which is a very great point. This is what St. Teresa of Ávila meant when she said: "Those from whom I receive the greatest consolation and encouragement are those whom I know to be dwelling in paradise." And St. Gregory the Great, in this very connection, makes a striking remark: "If," he says, "you love the good that you see in another, you make it your own."

We have heard the unbeliever Goethe complaining of the depressing spectacle of human mediocrity and failure. Another unbeliever arrived at a very different conclusion through reading the lives of the saints.

The French philosopher Ernest Renan thought that a prison cell in company with the *Acta Sanctorum* ("Acts of the Saints") produced by the Bollandists[18] would be a

---

17 Blessed John Henry Newman, *Apologia pro Vita Sua* (New York: Longmans, Green, 1908), 241–42.

18 The Bollandists are an association of historians, philologists, and other scholars who have studied and documented the lives of the saints since the early seventeenth century. The *Acta Santorum*, a collection

veritable paradise. He acknowledged that the records of saintliness had this value: that they put misanthropy to flight and deepen our appreciation of our fellow men. If "the world assumes a different aspect because of the presence of one genuine saint," our opinion of the world assumes a different complexion through contact and familiarity with the lives of the saints.

Newman remarked that the evils of life impress us with a ghastly sense of God's absence from His own creation; and the heroism of the saints impresses us with a cheerful sense of God's presence in His own creation.

THE CHALLENGE OF THE SAINTS

St. John Chrysostom assures us that on the Day of Judgment the bad will be accused by the very presence of the good; the cruel will be condemned by the memory of the merciful and kind; the fierce will be reproached by the very sight of the gentle; and so on. But the commemoration of the saints is a challenging sort of thing even here below—a thing calculated to reproach our timidity and slackness and to disturb our lukewarm complacency. Each single one of them is a vindicator who strikes a blow in defense of the reign of goodness and generosity upon our earth and recalls to our minds the meaning of words like "heroism," "self-sacrifice," "service," and more.

Indeed, our opinion of our fellowmen depends not

---

of documents relating to the lives of the saints, is their most important publication. It has come to number 63 volumes with a reference supplement. The association takes its name from Fr. Jean van Bolland (1596–1665), a Flemish Jesuit priest at Antwerp who edited the first volume of the *Acta*.

only on the kind of company we keep, but on the kind of books we read. After all, books are very like people. With some we feel at our best; with others we feel at our worst.

Some have the power to awaken in us all that is most wholesome and generous. Others, again, summon to the surface of the mind those elements of our fallen nature that, like the sewage drains, are best kept underground. Some act like a stimulant filling us with kindly and generous sentiments. Others act like a detergent purging us of all trustfulness and faith.

To an uncanny degree our estimation of human beings is dependent upon the samples of those exhibited in the pages of books. Close contact with the pride-stricken literature of the age makes us begin to wonder whether there is any modesty left in the world. If society has a bad name, the society novelist is certainly in part to blame; and those works of fiction, dictated by a sex-ridden fancy, that deluge the market imperceptibly create the impression that vileness is the order of the day.

Thank God, however, there are books and books. The French artist Edmé Bouchardon used to say: "When I read Homer I feel as though I were twenty feet high." Our own poet, John Keats, experienced the same wholesome elevation of mind "on first looking into Chapman's Homer":

> Then felt I like some watcher of the skies
> When a new planet swims into his ken;
> Or like stout Cortez when with eagle eyes
> He stared at the Pacific . . .[19]

---

19 John Keats, "On first looking into Chapman's Homer," in *The Complete*

And if a record of heroic deeds that is largely a work of imagination can thus expand the heart and ennoble the mind, what is likely to be the effect on us of contemplating the real achievements of the saints—those splendid pillars that tower upward and remind us of our dignity and destiny?

The German Church historian Johann Adam Möhler thus described the effect upon himself of reading the lives of the saints: "I found myself wondering at their great deeds, penetrated by the greatness of soul they displayed." And he added: "So would it be, I think, with the majority of men, if they did but give time to the perusal of those splendid memorials of the Christian past."

At any rate, there are plenty of saints. The Bollandists deal with some thirty or forty thousand of them; but St. John saw them as a vast multitude "which no man could number" (Rv 7:9). All Saints' Day is the festival of all those unknown warriors, those glorious patterns of Christ whose lives were completely hidden in God.

Those dead saints are a constant and needed reminder to us that the world in which we live is peopled by living ones; and this realization is a comfort, a real antidote to our pessimism. "Among us," wrote the Russian author Fydor Dostoyevsky in *The Brothers Karamazov*, "there is sin, injustice and temptation; but somewhere on earth there is someone holy, someone exalted. He has the truth; he knows the truth."

Poetical Works of John Keats (New York: Houghton, Mifflin, 1900), 15.

A WONDERFUL WORLD OF ROMANCE

HOWEVER puzzling our holy religion may be to the outer world, our separated brethren have, at any rate, a strong conviction that it does contain unmistakable elements of romance. If a novel is written against a religious background, the religion chosen is almost sure to be the Catholic religion.

If a garden is to figure in the book, it will very likely be a monastery garden. And if bells are going to ring, they will be convent bells. The writers may not be Catholics, but they are artists, and the artist in them is their guide.

Art, indeed, for many hundreds of years exhausted itself in depicting the splendors and glories of Catholicism. And even in these latter days, there is hardly a single painter of note who has not fallen under its spell and paid some tribute to its romance.

It is impossible to attend a season of Grand Opera without being confronted, night after night, with the customs and devotions of Catholics. *Romeo and Juliet* has its friar, and an excellent one at that. Rimsky Korsakov's *Boris* has two who are not quite so edifying. Joseph Conrad's *Romance* has a whole background of friars.

SAINTLY CHIVALRY

This religion, which was the religion of all the great poets and artists, the religion of the jesters and troubadours, is also the religion of the saints; and no novel was ever so romantic as some of their lives. It is no wonder that when St. Ignatius of Loyola called loudly for romances and was given the lives of the saints instead, he found them equally thrilling. So true it is that virtue produces far more interesting and romantic characters than vice. The account of St. Madeleine Sophie's life says that she had all the daring and adventurous courage of the knights of old, and we can quite believe it.

The knights fought with robbers and tyrants and giants. The saints fought with the Devil, the world, and the flesh. Both knights and saints leave home and country: the first in search of adventure, the second in quest of penance and peace.

"Come and see the tents of the soldiers of Christ; come and see their order of battle; they fight every day, and every day defeat and immolate the passions that assail us"—thus St. John Chrysostom describes the monastic orders of his day. The emperor Charlemagne called the abbots of his empire the *Chevaliers de l'Eglise*, the "Chivalry of the Church." The French historian Charles Forbes René de Montalembert says: "That comparison between the two knighthoods, lay and monastic, is . . . the everyday language of the history of the religious orders, and of the biography of those saints who have founded and illustrated them."[20]

---

20 All the quotes in this paragraph appear in [Charles Forbes René]

Just as the chivalry of the world had for its heroes Amadis of Gaul, Arthur, Tristan, Lancelot, Palmeron, Turpin, and the rest, so Anthony, Benedict, Anselm, Hildebrand, Thomas à Becket and the others figure in the chivalry of the Church. The exploits of the former are for the most part legendary, and in some cases the very existence of the hero is problematical. But when we have stripped even St. Patrick of the legends that have gathered about his person, there is enough and more than enough left to furnish material for a real drama.[21]

Didn't St. Teresa of Ávila as a young girl love to "dress up" in her father's coat-of-mail? This was done as a penance certainly. But considering the brave and knightly character of the saint, we may be sure that she found an inspiration in it.

The "Paladins of the Round Table" is the name that St. Francis of Assisi gave to his followers. Thomas of Celano says of Francis that in his youth he used to dream that his father's shop was full of shields and lances and all the equipment of the knight-errant; and St. Bonaventure likens his stigmata to the emblazonry of the secular warrior.

There is certainly no doubt about the romanticism of St. Francis. He stripped himself of everything; execrated

---

Comte de Montalembert, *The Monks of the West: From Saint Benedict to St. Bernard* (Boston: Patrick-Donahoe, 1872), 16–17. Here Montalembert paraphrases Chrysostom's observations in his 69th and 70th homilies on the Gospel of Matthew.

21 See, for example, John Edward Beahn, *A Man Cleansed by God: A Novel Based on the Life of Saint Patrick* (repr., Charlotte, N.C.: TAN Books, 2013).

money and took poverty for his bride; talked to the birds; reformed the wolf; claimed the moon for his sister and the sun for his brother; discovered a relationship with fire, with the wind, and with water; and he died on the floor saying, "Welcome, Brother Death." Indeed, as his biographer G. K. Chesterton says, "The amazing vividness with which he stamped himself on the memory and imagination of mankind is very largely due to the fact that he was seen again and again under such *dramatic* conditions."[22]

The English poet Francis Thompson thus writes of St. Ignatius: "With 'Amadis de Gaul' still in his head, he resolved to 'watch his arms' at the Church of Our Lady of Montserrat. . . . Never had religious order such chivalric birth. For on that night, one may say, was born . . . the Company of Jesus, the Free-Lances of the Church."[23]

ROMANTIC ADVENTURES AND EXPLOITS

We may read George Anson's *Voyage Round the World* or Captain James Cook's or Richard Hakluyt's entire collection of *Voyages,* and we shall find nothing so exciting as the story of St. Francis Xavier's voyage to the Indies. Scurvy and fever followed the stagnating of the water and the putrefying of the meat, but he converted his cabin into an infirmary and slept and ate on deck, jammed in the narrow vessel among the passengers who numbered over a thousand persons. He preached; he catechized; he made even the sailors stop swearing; and he lived on

---

22 G. K. Chesterton, *St. Francis of Assisi* (Garden City, N.Y.: Doubleday, 1946), 131, emphasis added.

23 Francis Thompson, *Life of St. Ignatius Loyola* (London: Burns, Gates & Washbourne, 1909), 17–18.

charity during the whole of a voyage that lasted for thirteen months.

Daniel Defoe's immortal *Robinson Crusoe* is largely a work of imagination. But what romantic tales could be written round the authentic facts of the lives of the ancient solitaries and hermits—the pillar saints, for example! Simeon, their pioneer, spent the last nineteen years of his life fifty-four feet above the ground, on a narrow platform with no protection except a rail to keep him from falling off during sleep. And besides these Stylites, as they were called, there were whole groups of solitaries (the *Spelaiotai*) who lived in caverns. Others (the *Gyrovagi*) who, impressed by the detachment of a Master who had nowhere to rest His head, dedicated themselves to a life of vagabondage, wandering from place to place, settling in and attaching themselves to no locality.[24]

The *Dendritai*—so called because they lived in trees—are in a large class by themselves. What child has not thrilled at the thought of Peter Pan and Wendy? And yet here is the thing in actual life.

St. Bavon, the patron of Ghent, is one such. As Duke of Brabant he lived an indifferent sort of worldly life. Being converted by St. Amand of Maestrich, he gave his possessions to the poor, entered a monastery, and then desiring a more complete seclusion, withdrew into a hollow tree in the depth of the forest and there passed the remainder of his life.

---

24 "Stylite" comes from the Greek word for "pillar"; *spelaiotai* comes from the Greek word for "cave"; *gyrovagi* comes from the Late Latin word for "circle wandering"; and *dendritai* (noted in the following paragraph) from the Greek word for "tree."

Our own English saint St. Simon Stock is so-called because, at the age of twelve, he chose for his dwelling a great hollow oak in a wood near Aylesford in Kent and lived there until he was called by God to join the Carmelites. It is well known that Croyland Abbey was built on the site of St. Guthlac's hermitage in one of the fens of Lincolnshire. Guthlac had been a highway robber, and after his conversion he lived on the banks of a desolate marsh with no companions except the birds and waterfowl. "Good Companions" these birds were because they used to perch on his shoulder as he worked and nestle in the folds of his cloak when the weather was cold.

DRAMATIC EPISODES

How dramatic was the conversion of Jacopone da Todi! He was a sinful man of the world married to a saintly wife. They were together one day watching a tournament when the grandstand collapsed. He was unhurt, but when he reached his wife's side, he saw that she was fatally injured.

He tore open her dress to give her air and saw that she was wearing a hair shirt. At the same moment, she drew her last breath. This incident and its sequel has been often described, but by none better than by the French scholar Frédéric Ozanam:

> This sudden death, these austere habits in one brought up in all the luxury of wealth, the absolute certainty that he alone was guilty of the sins which the hair shirt was intended to expiate, struck

> the lawyer of Todi as if by a thunderbolt. . . . After several days of gloomy stupefaction, he sold all his goods and distributed the money among the poor. He was seen in the churches and streets clothed in rags. . . . These eccentricities . . . served to conceal the first throes of a magnificent repentance.[25]

Even a man like Matthew Arnold was profoundly stirred by this drama of repentance. It was about this famous poet and follower of St. Francis that he wrote the lines beginning: "In his light youth amid the festal throng."[26]

How dramatic is the story of St. Augustine's conversion!

> Behold, I heard a voice from some neighbor's house like that of a boy or girl (though I knew not which), in a singing tune saying and often repeating: *Take up and read, take up and read.* At that my countenance instantly changed. I began very carefully to consider whether children were accustomed in any kind of play to sing these words, but I couldn't remember ever having heard them. So quickly I went again to the place where I had laid the Apostle's book. I snatched it up, I opened it, and in silence I read that chapter: *Not in reveling and drunkenness, not in debauchery and licentiousness,*

---

25 Frédéric Ozanam, *The Franciscan Poets in Italy of the Thirteenth Century*, trans. A. E. Nellen and N. C. Craig (New York: Charles Scribner's, 1914), 193–94.

26 Matthew Arnold, "Austerity of Poetry," in *The Works of Arnold Matthew*, Vol. II, *Poems* (London: Macmillan, 1903), 121.

> *not in quarreling and jealousy. But put on the Lord Jesus Christ* [Rom 13:13–14]. No further word I read; nor did I need to read. For instantly all the darkness of doubt vanished away.[27]

Then there is St. John Gualbert. Believing himself bound in honor to avenge his brother's murder, he searches incessantly for the assassin and confronts him at last on Good Friday. The man falls on his knees and begs for mercy in the name of Christ's passion. St. John pardons him and then goes off to Vallombrosa—that Vallombrosa whose autumn leaves Milton mentions in his *Paradise Lost.*[28]

St. Severus of Ravenna was a poor weaver and married. One day he puts on his coat and tells his wife that he will run along to the cathedral to see them electing a new bishop. "Go along then," says the sarcastic wife, "and perhaps you will be elected yourself."

He goes, and sure enough he is elected. The neighbors rush home to tell the wife. "A likely story," she says; "a man who tosses the shuttle would make a fine bishop." And indeed a fine bishop he made.

These are the sort of episodes that dramatists would like to put on the stage or screen if they only knew how to do it. Perhaps if these things were done for a motive other than a religious motive, the world would get really excited about them.

St. Clare eloped to the cloister. As Chesterton says, "She escaped through a hole in the wall, fled through a

---

27 See Augustine of Hippo, *Confessions,* V, 12.

28 See John Milton, *Paradise Lost,* Bk. I, l. 303.

wood, and was received at midnight by the light of torches."[29] Here is "a wall," "a wood," "midnight" and "torches," and yet people are not moved all because there is a cloister as well.

Chesterton continues: "If the girl had become a bride instead of a nun, practically the whole modern world would have made her a heroine."[30] If there is an element of romance in going to dance at midnight with bare arms, is there no poetry at all to be seen in the contemplative who gets up to pray at midnight with bare feet?

COLORFUL CHARACTERS

Benvenuto Cellini sat up all night, with anxiety in his eyes, to watch his statue of Perseus hardening in the furnace—and much has been made of the fact. But St. Robert Bellarmine sat up all night with even greater anxiety in his eyes to watch St. Aloysius, whom he loved like a son. St. Athanasia and St. Aurelia concealed their sex; St. Euphrosyna, disguised as a hermit, lived for years beside her own father without his recognizing her; St. John Chalybita hid his identity from his mother; and St. Alexis passed himself off as a servant and was treated as such by his own parents.

What a tremendous fuss is made, and how busy the reporters are, when, as sometimes happens, someone in our modern world through sheer love of notoriety or eccentricity attempts to do just this sort of thing! That modern world has acclaimed the heroism of Florence

29 Chesterton, 162.

30 Chesterton, 163.

Nightingale, known as the founder of the Red Cross. But it has taken no heed at all of St. Camillus of Lellis, who centuries earlier founded the first such ministry, which included the first field medical unit.

Saints are known to have written resolutions in their own blood. St. Mary Magdalen of Pazzi, for example, thus wrote her famous resolution: "All for God and nothing for self." A recent book on Ireland reveals the detail that the Ulster Volunteers who were enrolled to resist the Home Rule Bill recorded their oaths in exactly the same ink. Yet possibly those who applaud the "heroism" of the Orangemen would be the very first to deride the fanaticism of the saints.

Among the curiosities of great men, it is carefully recorded how, in a fit of mental abstraction, Church of Ireland Archbishop Richard Whately devoured sixteen plovers' eggs out of the eighteen set out on the table for the use of his guests. Edward Gibbon, the historian, worked at his great book on the banks of Lake Geneva without once looking at the lake. Andrew Miller, busy with Brian Walton's Polyglot Bible while sitting at a window overlooking the Strand in London, did not even look up to see the restoration procession of King Charles II going past. And so on and so on.

But this is just the type of person that some of the saints were. St. Vincent de Paul ate a couple of eggs that the cook had forgotten to boil. St. Bernard drank off a glass of oil given to him, mistaking it for wine. And St. Thomas walked on the banks of Lake Geneva without even seeing the lake. St. Alonzo Rodriguez ate a plate of fungus served up in mistake for mushrooms. St. Aloysius while a novice was never once aware of the novice master's visits to his room during the meditation.

THRILLING SCENES

Truly, everything agreeable is to be found in the lives of the saints, including thrills. St. Raymond of Pennafort was forbidden to leave the island of Majorca and could find no one willing to convey him to Barcelona. So he walked boldly into the sea, spread his cloak upon the waves, tied one corner of it to his staff for a sail and, having made the sign of the cross, stepped upon it without fear—and away he went doing the sixty leagues in six hours.

When Placid fell into the lake and was carried far out of his depth, St. Benedict gave Brother Maurus an obedience to go and fish him out. Maurus never hesitated, but ran as fast as his legs could carry him right out into the middle and brought the little boy back in his arms. It was only when he was once more on dry land that he suddenly remembered that he had been walking on water.

Who has not been thrilled in reading the account of the mishap that befell the manuscript of Thomas Carlyle's *French Revolution* and of the author's courage in making good the loss? The manuscript of the first volume was sent to his friend John Stuart Mill, the philosopher and political economist, for correction.

> One evening . . . Carlyle was seated with his wife, when "a rap was heard at the door . . . and Mill entered deadly pale, and at first unable to speak." "Why, Mill," said Carlyle, "what ails ye, man?" . . . Mill was led to a seat, and at last told in broken

> sentences how the manuscript, left about too carelessly after it had been read, was "except four or five bits of leaves, irrevocably annihilated"—burnt by a servant girl. . . .
>
> Carlyle, after enduring agony . . . determined that he could still write a book on the French Revolution, and would do it; he felt as if his Invisible Schoolmaster had torn his copybook when he showed it, and said: "No, boy! Thou must write it better."[31]

Equally thrilling is Eadmer's account of the accident that befell St. Anselm's famous argument for the existence of God. The saint had applied his whole mind to it for days together. When at last he saw it clearly, he was filled with joy and made haste to commit it to writing.

The wax tablets were then given into the charge of one of the monks. But when they were wanted they were missing; and although a diligent search was made, they were never found. There was nothing to do except to sit down once again and apply his mind to the subject; and this Anselm did with complete success.

The argument was then written on fresh tablets and given into safer keeping. But, again, when it was wanted, it was found that the tablets were broken to pieces. With the greatest of difficulty the saint assembled the fragments for greater security.

31 G.T.B., "Introduction," in Thomas Carlyle, *The French Revolution: A History* (London: Ward, Lock & Co., 1888), [iv–v].

THE ROMANTICISM OF HOLINESS

Few characters of romantic fiction have received greater attention from writers than that of Griselda, a character from European folklore known for her patience. Boccaccio, Chaucer, Petrarch, Dekker, and Goldoni each treated the character in his own way. And in the Middle Ages there were upwards of twenty different popular versions of the figure in use at the same time.

Yet St. Elizabeth of Hungary was the "patient Griselda" in real life. This princess was so reduced in the end that she could find no door open to receive her in the town where formerly she had been received with acclamation. "Thus she, who had entertained thousands of poor, could find no entertainment or harbor; and she who had been a mother to so many infants and orphans, was glad to beg alms for her own, and to receive it from her enemies."[32]

After five years of happy married life, she lost her husband, her position, and her estate; and yet she did not even complain. Dying at the age of twenty-three, she left behind a son, Herman, who later became a page at the Court of Queen Blanche of France. "Where did your mother kiss you, child?" Blanche used to ask Herman. And when he pointed to his forehead, she would kiss him there.

One might continue almost indefinitely recalling those dramatic episodes that have been the inspiration of the highest Christian art. St. Monica and St. Augustine at the window of Ostia looking out over the sea; St.

---

32 Rev. Alban Butler, *The Lives of the Fathers, Martyrs, and Other Principle Saints* (Dublin: James Duffy, 1866), XI, 320.

Bonaventure hanging the cardinal's hat upon a tree and then going on with the washing of the dishes;[33] St. Dominic's table served by the angels wearing aprons; all the bells ringing of their own accord at the death of St. Maurus; the rock opening up and giving a shelter to St. Ariadna flying from her persecutors; St. Benedict preaching to the ladies of the world, St. Francis preaching to the birds, St. Anthony preaching to the fishes, and the first Dominican Friars preaching from books that Our Lady herself held open before them.

When St. Gertrude wrote her *Herald of Divine Love,* she presented it to Our Lord, who pressed it to His heart in order, as He said, to penetrate it through and through with His own spirit.

A butterfly strongly marked with the Dominican black and white that fluttered round St. Rose of Lima confirmed her in her desire to be a tertiary of St. Dominic. Later she built a tiny hermitage for herself made of twigs and palm leaves and furnished with little pictures. This garden cell became her life.

The birds perched on her hands and shoulders, and she played with a ball with the Divine Child. And she is unique among the saints in that she chose the mosquitoes as her favorite pets. They never harmed her, and daily she summoned them to the cell and bade them join in their own way in singing the Divine Office.

---

33 When St. Bonaventure was first appointed cardinal, the papal nuncios who were sent from Rome to bring him his hat and other signs of his new dignity found him on the road, where he had stopped for a meal. He was washing dishes. In his humility, he asked them to hang the hat on a nearby tree until he had finished his menial task.

Such is the romanticism of holiness. It is no wonder that Alban Butler says that "the lives of the saints furnish the Christian with a daily spiritual entertainment, which is not less agreeable than affecting and instructive."[34]

34 Butler, I, iv.

THE SAINTS IN HISTORY

"SO GREAT [are] the charms of history that, on every subject and whatever dress it wears, it always pleases and finds readers."[35] And yet what reader of history, however fascinated, doesn't feel the one-sidedness of the document? The Dominican orator Henri-Dominique Lacordaire called it the "rich treasury of man's dishonor." And in introducing his own volumes, historian John Richard Green roundly denounces the stereotyped partiality of historians that has made written history the biography of a few heroes who were not so very heroic after all. For indeed:

> The drying up a single tear has more
> Of honest fame, than shedding seas of gore.[36]

Although fame is courted and applauded, she is seldom just. The greatest sacrifices and the truest acts of heroism never reach her ears, are never published by her trumpet. "It is," says Green, "the reproach of historians that they have too often turned history into a mere record of the butchery of men by their fellow men."[37]

---

35 Butler, I, ix.

36 From the poem "Don Juan" by Lord Byron.

37 John Richard Green, *A Short History of the English People* (London:

Edward Gibbon, again, quoting from Voltaire, called it "little more than the register of the crimes, follies, and misfortunes of mankind."[38] One of the earliest of our Church historians, Socrates, acknowledged that if the people who figure in its pages had acted justly and decently, history would be reduced to a collection of mere dates. No doubt this is what he had in mind who said: "Happy is the nation that has no history."

Indeed, how much misery the world would have been spared if the rewards of fame were reserved only for those who really deserved them! "What," asks Alban Butler, "are the boasted triumphs of an Alexander or a Caesar, but a series of successful plunders, murders, and other crimes?"[39] The power exemplified in the pages of history is mainly the power of brute force, and its idols, when closely inspected, turn out to have feet of clay—and commonly very dirty clay at that.

The exploits of Cyrus the king of Persia have been extolled by ancient historians. But Herodotus tells us that when he had been defeated and slain in battle with Queen Tomyris, she caused a vessel to be filled with human blood, and throwing the head of Cyrus into it, she said: "Now at length you can drink your fill."

The achievements of the heroes of history, when stripped of their glamour, are seen to be deserving of

---

MacMillan, 1902), I, xxiv.

38 Edward Gibbon, *The History of the Decline and Fall of the Roman Empire* (New York: Fred De Fau, 1906), I, 98; paraphrasing Voltaire, "*L'histoire n'est que le tableau des crimes et des malheurs*" ("History is but the record of crimes and misfortunes") in *L'Ingénu*, chap. 6.

39 Butler, I, ix.

abhorrence rather than of praise. Apart from the tremendous scale on which they were carried out, they have very little to recommend them.

Diodorus the Greek historian relates a very instructive incident in the life of Alexander the Great. A pirate was captured and brought before the king. "What right have you to infest the seas?" Alexander asked.

"I have as much right as you have," the pirate answered. "But because I do on a small scale what you do on a big scale, I am called a pirate, and you are called a mighty conqueror."

THE ENCOURAGING SPECTACLE OF THE SAINTS

It is no wonder that the British statesman William Gladstone could write: "The history of nations is a melancholy chapter; that is, the history of governments is one of the most immoral parts of that history."[40]

Therefore we may well be grateful that secular history is not the whole of history, that there is another side to it besides the "drum and trumpet" side. If the object of all historical studies is to converse with the greatest minds of the best ages, we must evidently look for something besides a catalog of battles and sieges.[41]

Fortunately, we are able to do so. If history is the

40 Quoted in John Morley, *The Life of William Ewart Gladstone* (London: MacMillan, 1922), II, 779.

41 We should note that in the years since Fr. Roche wrote this book, many historians have departed from the traditional focus on political and military history, examining instead the historical contours of social and cultural life.

"mistress of life," as Cicero calls it; and if history is "moral philosophy exemplified in the lives and actions of mankind";[42] then we may congratulate ourselves that, against the depressing background of secular history, there stands out serene and consoling the contribution to history which we call the lives of the saints. They present to us the most encouraging of all spectacles: that of heroes and conquerors victorious in the service of a really good cause.

Here, at any rate, is a tribute paid to virtue and self-sacrifice. Here, some attention is given to those who restrained their passions and devoted themselves to the betterment of their fellowmen. Here, man is seen not at his very worst, but at his very best. And here, some conception begins to float before the mind of what human nature is capable of, under the influence of divine grace.

Charity, pity, generosity, self-sacrifice, heroism—these are the ingredients of sacred history. They provide us with memorials of the dead that are neither scandalous nor disgusting, but rather exemplary, edifying and above all elevating—that is to say, calculated to deepen our pride in our own species.

In the long history of the Church the lives of eminent holy people have never failed. Sanctity can no more help welling up from her than can the water from a fountain. The source of all that is virtuous in the world about us is to be found in the heart of the Church.

"Let no one deny to the Catholic Church one great

42 Butler, ix, citing Cicero, l. 2 *de Orat.* c. 9, and G. J. Voss, *Ars Historica*, cap. 5 (1623).

note of the true Church, namely, the power to breed saints." This is the testimony of a non-Catholic, the late English writer Augustine Birrell. "The Catholic Church," writes Belloc, "makes men. By which I do not mean boasters and swaggerers, nor bullies nor ignorant fools . . . but men, human beings different from the beasts, capable of firmness and discipline and recognition; accepting death; tenacious."[43]

Indeed, it is remarkable that the most relaxed and therefore most dangerous periods of the Church's history have commonly been the most fertile in the production of heroic souls. Time and again when abuses have been rampant, God has raised up those "cohorts of the virtuous" to check the march of the Evil One. At such moments the All-Powerful allows the law of equilibrium to operate.

As a reparation for the sins of the many, He claims the mortifications and prayers of the generous few. When the pendulum inclines too much to the side of evil, He excites the ardor of His servants, thus employing, as has been said, the tactics by which He subdued the hordes led by the rebel angels. The note of sanctity in the Church is in fact closely allied to the note of indefectibility.[44]

---

43 Hilaire Belloc, *The Path to Rome* (New York: Longmans, Green, 1902), 351.

44 In traditional Catholic teaching, the "notes" of the Church refer to the Church's properties or essential attributes. The "note of sanctity" refers to the Church's holiness; the "note of indefectibility" refers to her imperishable nature. "The Church is indefectible, that is, she remains and will remain the Institution of Salvation, founded by Christ, until the end of the world": Ludwig Ott, *Fundamentals of Catholic Dogma* (repr., Charlotte, N.C.: TAN Books, 2013), 296.

THE CHURCH CHERISHES VIRTUE

Vendier, one of the members of the Italian secret societies known as the Carbonari, wrote to a fellow Freemason: "The best weapon for striking at the heart of the Church is corruption. Create vicious hearts, and you will make short work of Catholicism."

But the discernment of holiness, the swift and instinctive detection of virtue, is also one of the notes of the Church. It is nothing short of a divine faculty. "If," wrote the historian Jaime Balmez, "you are a man of high merit untarnished by misconduct, the Church will look upon you as a great man."[45]

In the eyes of the Church, at least, it is still "worth that makes the man." She welcomes a display of worth wherever she finds it, whether in unpretentious, humble people such as St. Zita and St. Benedict Joseph, or in public characters such as St. Ferdinand and St. Edward the Confessor.

That is to say, she honors and preserves in her annals the name and memory of those whom the secular historian ignores. She has been as indefatigable in preserving the memory of good lives as the secular historian has been in preserving the memory of bad lives. And for this, civilization and society owe a deep debt to the Church.

This was well understood in days gone by. Hence we find kings and princes petitioning for the canonization of saints. For example—and there is some consolation in the

---

45 Jaime Balmez, "Society Mainly Indebted to the Catholic Church for the Progress It Has Made in Political Liberty," *New Zealand Tablet*, Oct. 18, 1873, 6.

fact—our own Henry VIII urged Pope Leo X to canonize St. Colette the Poor Clare. With all their shortcomings, these rulers felt that every canonization is a real compliment to our human nature; that in honoring the saints we are honoring ourselves; and that the public advertisement of their virtues is a tremendous social advantage.

The mischief of some of these "splendid" biographies of great people is that they are apt to create a kind of false conscience. In them we find men judged as statesmen, or politicians, or soldiers alone, and not as men, as fathers, as husbands, and so on. Certainly, all our ethical notions would be turned upside down if vicious men and women were allowed to monopolize the entire field of history.

By herself entering that field, by cherishing the virtues of mankind, the Church does much to check in us that fascination we feel for what is wrong. We do not admire crime; but we are rather fond of reading about it. The enterprises of burglars and criminals exercise a great ascendancy over the imagination. Although the exhilaration that a detective story, or the career of great historical personages such as Napoleon, brings us is innocent enough in itself, yet there is always a danger of our acquiring what the English essayist Joseph Addison called "a leaning towards all grandiose forms of vice and a contempt only for the squalid kinds."

At any rate, since the real object of literature, history included, is to preserve the moral and intellectual sanity of mankind, literature must never be allowed to become the triumphant record of those who hated virtue and loved vice. And the literature of sanctity sees to that. "Goodness, Goodness, Goodness," was the favorite aspiration of St. Bruno; and it is the note that runs through the lives of all God's servants.

Evil was their sole aversion. "If," said St. Ignatius Loyola, "I can keep only one soul out of mortal sin, my life will have been a success." One bad word overheard in conversation kept St. Mary Magdalen of Pazzi awake all night.

"Rather death than sin," said St. Dominic Savio. "Rather hell than sin," said St. John Chrysostom. "Only let there be no sin," said St. Philip Neri. St. Catherine of Genoa, having been shown the malice of mortal sin, swooned away and would have died had she not been supported by God. Even Goethe could not deny this merit to the saints: "If without beauty," so he said, "they are always good."

REAL MAKERS OF HISTORY

In the calendar of the saints we find a multitude whose very names are suggestive of momentous events, who were real makers of history and of large-scale history at that. A fourteenth-century chronicler says of St. Bridget of Sweden that on the day of her birth, a priest heard a supernatural voice saying: "Tonight there will be born a child to whose words the whole world will one day listen." Equally momentous was the nativity of many another saint.

St. Augustine, for example, embodies in his own person that disturbed, uneasy period when paganism and Christianity were engaged in a final conflict. St. Telemachus by his heroic sacrifice put an end to an abuse which was the scandal of Christendom. St. Bernard's preaching of the crusade emptied the towns and castles of Europe to such an extent that the ordinary business of life was suspended or relegated to the womenfolk. The hills and valleys of Europe echoed the strains of the war song which he is said to have composed for the occasion:

> Before the morning light I'll come
> With Magdalen to find,
> With sighs and tears, my Savior's tomb . . .

Mary Magdalene was, of course, the patron of the crusade.

St. Bernard, in fact, was in a sense the dictator of his age—the "Oracle of Europe," as he has been called. Across the vista of seven centuries we see him commanding kings, directing popes, compelling nations, directing the men and things among which he lived. In short, we see him as one of the greatest statesmen of history.

Thus a non-Catholic American writer has written:

> Surely we must accept [St. Bernard] as quite the most eminent and governing man in the Europe of his time; whose temper had in it a remarkable combination of sweetness and tenderness, with practical sagacity, devout consecration, a dauntless courage, and a terrible intensity; whose word carried with it a sovereign stress surpassing that of any other, whose hand most effectively molded history.[46]

Of St. Thomas à Becket, Lord John Campbell, in his *Lives of the Lord Chancellors,* says that he was one of the

46 Richard Salter Storrs, *Bernard of Clairvaux: The Times, the Man, and His Work* (New York: Charles Scribner's Sons, 1901), 574

most distinguished men of any race that this island has yet produced. St. Thomas à Becket fought for a principle of the utmost consequence to society as a whole. He fought in order to free religion from the tyranny of the civil power. "The spirit against which he fought was the spirit which either openly or secretly believes the Church to be an institution merely human and therefore naturally subjected, as an inferior, to the processes of the monarch's, or, worse, the politician's law."[47]

How profound and far-reaching was the influence that the example of St. Anthony the Patriarch of the monastic life exercised on society! If ever there was a man who dominated history, dictated to the future, molded the lives of generations yet unborn, it was surely this man. Intent at first only upon the salvation of his own soul, he initiated one of the most amazing movements that history records.

There were certainly hermits before his time. But he is their recognized leader, and the monks of the desert, who at one time numbered hundreds of thousands, looked upon him as the father of monasticism. Indeed, he is the father of the technical religious life in every shape and form. That is to say, no Christian name has inspired greater heroism or been productive of deeper and more lasting results.

47 John Campbell, *Lives of the Lord Chancellors* (London: John Murray, 1868).

SMALL CAUSES, MOMENTOUS CONSEQUENCES

The vocation of St. Anthony exemplifies a truth that runs right through history: the truth, namely, that slight and insignificant causes have their sequel in momentous events. "How great a forest is set ablaze by a small fire!" (Jas 3:5). A mere casual remark introduced into France the practice of dueling, which in the end cost the country more blood than twenty battles: "Go and settle your quarrels among yourselves," said François de Bassompierre, the Minister under Cardinal Richelieu.

So a text dropped by accident from the lips of a preacher sent St. Anthony into the desert and produced the worldwide movement associated with his name. "Go, sell what you have, and give to the poor . . . and come, follow Me" (Mk 10:21).

Who could exaggerate the social blessings that came to society through the Pax (peace) of St. Benedict, the poverty of St. Francis of Assisi, and the charity of St. Vincent de Paul! Not only has the Benedictine Order given twenty-six popes to the Church and five thousand saints to the world; it brought the greater part of Europe under cultivation. And in a lawless and factious age, it impressed upon the minds of men the important social truth that the arts of peace are more creditable and valuable to man than the arts of war.

The Order has been compared to a framework of living points on which was stretched the moral life of Europe during the Dark Ages. "As a code of laws," writes Abbot Francis Aidan Gasquet, the Rule of St. Benedict "has undoubtedly influenced Europe; and indeed there is probably no other book, save of course the Holy Bible, which with such certainty can be claimed as a chief factor in the work of European civilization."[48] "But for the monks," says Belloc, "we should all have fallen into barbarism."[49]

Of St. Francis it has been said that his life flashed like a tender beam of light across the dark background of his time. But there was nothing transitory about the influence of St. Francis. His example enriched the cause of humanitarianism for all time. He has been called the Father of the Renaissance, that is to say, of that authentic and Christian Humanism which was unfortunately displaced by its semi-pagan rival. And his poetry contributed enormously to the development and consolidation of the Italian language.

As for St. Vincent de Paul, it is to him that organized social service must look back as to its creator. Since his death there is scarcely a part of the habitable globe that has not benefited by the charity which he inspired.

THE HERITAGE OF MANKIND

That is why so many of the saints belong not to this or that locality, but to the whole world. Their influence has become the heritage of mankind.

St. Clare of Assisi advanced the cause of social equality by throwing open the monastic life to women of the humbler classes who previously were practically excluded.

---

48 Cardinal Francis Aidan Gasquet, "Introduction," in *The Rule of Saint Benedict*, trans. Francis Aidan Gasquet (New York: Cooper Square, 1966), ix.

49 Hilaire Belloc, *Europe and the Faith* (New York: Paulist, 1921), 187.

St. Anselm and others like him, by their heroic resistance to tyranny, contributed tremendously to the restoration of the subverted liberties of men. St. Charles Borromeo founded the Sunday school. The victory of Lepanto that is closely identified with the name of St. Pius V was a boon to civilization for which we in the West have never been sufficiently grateful or even appreciative.

Let us take the three saints mainly responsible for the conversion of Great Britain and Ireland. The average secular historian may have neither use nor time for saints, but he is bound to take notice of the civilizing effects of the mission of St. Patrick to Ireland. The historian Johann Döllinger writes:

> During the sixth and seventh centuries . . . the schools in the Irish cloisters were the most celebrated in all the West. . . . Whilst almost the whole of Europe was desolated by war, peaceful Ireland, free from the invasions of external foes, opened to the lovers of learning and piety a welcome asylum. The strangers who visited the island, not only from the neighboring shores of Britain, but also from the most remote nations of the Continent, received from the Irish people the most hospitable reception, a gratuitous entertainment, free instruction, and even the books that were necessary for their studies. . . . Many holy and learned Irishmen left their own country to . . . become the benefactors of almost every nation of Europe.[50]

50 Johann Joseph Ignaz von Döllinger, *A History of the Church*, Edward Cox, trans. (London: C. Dolman and T. Jones, 1840), II, 30–31.

Speaking of the sending of St. Augustine to England, Newman says:

> St. Gregory . . . who engaged in this sacred negotiation was led . . . to do a deed which resulted in surprising benefits to the whole of Christendom. Here lay the answer to the great problem which had so anxiously perplexed his mind. The old world was to pass away, and its wealth and wisdom with it; but these two islands were to be the storehouse of the past and the birthplace of the future. A divine purpose ruled his act of love towards the Anglo-Saxon race. . . . The seventh and eighth centuries are the glory of the Anglo-Saxon Church. . . . Amid the deep pagan woods of Germany and round about, the English Benedictine plied his axe and drove his plough . . . and then settling down as a colonist upon the soil, began to . . . lay the slow but sure foundations of the new civilization.[51]

"Columba," says the Duke of Argyll, "was an agent, and a principal agent, in one of the greatest events the world has ever seen, namely, the conversion of the northern nations. . . . Christianity was not presented to [the Picts of Caledonia] in alliance with the impressive aspects of Roman civilization. The tramp of the Roman legions had never been heard in the Highland glens, nor had their clans ever seen with awe the Roman government. . . . All the more must we be ready to believe that

---

51 Newman, *The Rise and Progress of Universities; and, Benedictine Essays* (London: Basil Montague Pickering, 1872–3), 124, 128.

the man who, at such a time, planted Christianity successfully among them, must have been a man of powerful character and of splendid gifts."[52]

St. Margaret of Scotland became the nursing mother of its civilization. She was instrumental in lifting the people of her adoption to a height of culture and prosperity unknown before. And here is Bishop Felix Dupanloup's graphic account of what St. Joan of Arc did for France:

> When the tempest had burst, when fire had been set to the pile of faggots . . . when her last look across the rising flames rested on the cross of Jesus Christ . . . when the last cry of her heart and the last movement of those expiring lips had three times uttered that name of Eternal Love, Jesus; then, as at Calvary, the murderers wept. But the flames endeavored vainly to consume that heart, guarded as it was by virginal purity and one poor wooden cross. . . . Then the star re-ascended to heaven: the Divine signal was visible to all eyes: the people of France once more took heart: terror and disgrace dogged the footsteps of the foreigner on the soil of this country, until driven from province to province he disappeared at last beyond the seas. And France, while other nations fell, moved henceforward at the head of the people of Europe as queen of the civilized world. . . . Such was the fruit of this great sacrifice.[53]

---

52 Duke of Argyll, *Iona* (Edinburgh: David Douglas, 1889), 49, 52–53.

53 F. LaGrange, *Life of Monseigner Dupanloup, Bishop of Orleans* (repr., Kessinger, 2006), II.

THE UNSELFISHNESS OF THE SAINTS

SELFISHNESS is the blot that disfigures worldly greatness. To the darlings of history we can deny neither genius, energy, nor glory. But it is very disappointing to find so much genius, so much energy, and so much glory used up in order to decorate and perfume the career of one man.

"Great men," said Lord Acton, "are almost always bad men,"[54] and they were that because they were selfish men. Those names which dazzle us are almost all associated with a deplorable egotism. And it is rather a melancholy reflection that mankind insists upon awarding the chief place in its admiration to those who attained their selfish ends by a clever use of some of the worst qualities in human nature.

The ancient Greek historian Plutarch gave some very good advice to the Roman emperor Trajan: "Let your government commence in your breast, and lay the foundations of it in the command of your passions."[55] But

54 Letter of Lord Acton to Bishop Mandell Creighton, April 5, 1887, published in *Historical Essays and Studies*, J. N. Figgis and R. V. Laurence, eds. (London: Macmillan, 1907).

55 Quoted by John Langhorne and William Langhorne, "A Life of

what use did Trajan make of this advice? And what use was made of this sort of advice by any of the other Trajans of the world?

Napoleon acknowledged that the conquest of self is more creditable than the conquest of Europe. But he preferred the latter and easier sort of conquest. It is strange, indeed, that we who are disgusted when we find selfishness in a friend or acquaintance are rather fascinated when we find it seated on a throne or exercised in a grandiose and wholesale manner.

THE GLORY OF GOD AND THE WELFARE OF MAN

Now, varied as are the lives and characters of the saints, they are all made in the image and likeness of real unselfishness. Well instructed by the Gospel, and well trained in the school of Christian perfection, they were never content with loving God. They were not even content with loving their neighbor as themselves. They loved their neighbor more than they loved themselves.

Although they were occupied above all in securing for themselves a place in the kingdom of heaven, one and all were philanthropists in the best sense of the word. They sought the glory of God and they sought the welfare of man. They loved God much, and therefore much did they love their neighbor.

Indeed, in the case of some of them, pity for their fellowman may be said to have initiated the movement of grace that brought them to the perfect love of God. Thus

---

Plutarch," in *Plutarch's Lives*, trans. J. Langhorne and W. Langhorne (New York: Harper & Brothers, 1872), xv.

was it, for example, with both St. Romuald, the "Forgiving Knight" as he is called, and St. John Gualbert.

St. Augustine did not wish to go to heaven without his flock.

St. Dominic asked God to place him as a stone in the mouth of hell if that would keep souls from falling into it. Dominic's biographer Jordan of Saxony says of him that he received from the Most High the rare grace of being able to sorrow for those in trouble and affliction, even to the shedding of tears; and again, that nothing could disturb the even-temperedness of his soul except his quick sympathy with every kind of suffering.

Almost the very last words of Dominic were these: "I am going where I can serve you better." Thus, like St. Thérèse the Little Flower, he associated the notion of service with heaven itself.

One of the earliest biographers of St. Anthony of Padua declares that he died a martyr to his charity. Had he considered himself, he might have lived for many more years—many more, that is to say, than thirty-eight.

In his task of converting the 72,000 Protestants of the Chablais, St. Francis de Sales risked his life over and over again in crawling over glaciers and fording mountain torrents.

St. Catherine of Genoa "was so compassionate to all creatures that when an animal was killed or a tree cut down she could hardly bear to see them lose that life that God had given them."[56]

---

56 St. Catherine of Genoa, *Life and Doctrine of Saint Catherine of Genoa* (New York: Christian Press Association, 1907), 44.

SAVING SOULS AND BODIES

The Mirror of Perfection, a memoir of St. Francis by his disciple Brother Leo, recalled: "He prayed all night so that he thought not of rest or sleep but only how he might help to save the souls of others." "Give me souls!" was the great cry of the saints. And not only on souls did they have compassion, but on bodies as well.

St. Francis, for example, laid the foundations of a social revolution. He worked wonders in the direction of softening and humanizing mankind. His Third Order was perhaps one of the biggest attempts ever made to introduce more justice and fair play among men and to direct the sympathies of the world to the weak and the humble.

No one, God alone excepted, ever loved mankind as did the saints: "Weep with the unhappy" was the advice that St. Columba gave to his followers. "If pity were a sin," said St. Bernard, I could not help committing it." St. Hugh of Lincoln as bishop regularly brought the lepers into his room and washed their feet and conversed with them unknown to his attendants.

St. Peter Claver assisted at public executions, and he would hold the poor wretches close to his heart while the rope was being put around their neck. What tremendous charity and strength of mind St. Catherine of Siena must have had to be able to perform the same sort of ministry. She not only converted the young man who was condemned to death, but she stood with him on the scaffold and held his hand while the axe fell.

In truth, the saints saw God Himself in their fellow man, and they acted accordingly. St. John of the Cross, for example, was not at all surprised when he saw the stigmata appearing on the feet of the poor beggar whom he was washing. He simply looked up into his face and said: "So it is you, Lord." It is recorded of St. Adelaide, the wife of the emperor Lothaire, that she never forgot a kindness and never remembered an injury.

It was said of St. Francis de Sales that if you wanted a favor from him, you had only to do him a bad turn. He was certainly full of courtesy and consideration. When he took possession of his diocese, he found that the peasants were bound by an old feudal custom to take turns silencing the frogs while the bishop was having his siesta. He would have none of it, so that the custom was abolished and the frogs croaked to their hearts' content.

"Give not your time to any man," wrote Seneca, "because it is a gift so precious that the most grateful can never return it or give its equivalent." This is a fine pagan maxim that the saints turned inside out.

St. Teresa of Ávila, for example, was so incessantly occupied with the welfare of other people that she has been called the Mother of the Church. St. Philip Neri not only gave up hours of his time to his young men, but he was prepared, as he said, to let them break stones on his back in order to keep them out of mischief. The Curé of Ars heard confessions for sixteen hours a day, and this during nearly thirty years.

AVOIDING SPIRITUAL EGOTISM

How well the saints succeeded in avoiding that great peril of piety—spiritual egotism. The noted English theologian Father Frederick Faber points out that spirituality rather tends to become selfish. Devout people are apt to get wrapped up in themselves.

Outside the Church, this form of egotism has exalted itself into a regular system. The popular author Robert Louis Stevenson says of John Knox, the Calvinist clergyman who established the Protestant Reformation in Scotland: "There was in him a fatal preponderance of self. . . . Even in his imprudent relations with women, he had, from first to last, no worry except for his own good name."[57]

In his Anglican days John Henry Newman thus described the Evangelicals of his time: "[They] are taken up with their own feelings." "The inherent mischief of [their] system . . . I conceive to lie in its necessarily involving a continual self-contemplation and reference to self."[58]

Later, on reading *Life of Wesley* (the English founder of the Methodist movement), Newman wrote to his sister: "I do not like Wesley—putting aside his exceeding self-confidence, he seems to me to have a black self-will . . . which is very unamiable."[59]

---

57 The first sentence of this quote appears in Robert Louis Stevenson, "John Knox and His Relations to Women," in *Familiar Studies of Men and Books*, 13th ed. (London: Chatto & Windus, 1898), 393. The second sentence does not appear anywhere in the same essay; it seems to be the author's restatement of Stevenson's preceding sentence: "It is characteristic that we find him more alarmed for his own reputation than for the reputation of the women with whom he was familiar."

58 The first quote comes from Newman, "Lecture 13: On Preaching the Gospel," in *Lectures on the Doctrine of Justification* (London: Longmans, Green, 1908), 339. The second is found in Newman, "Self-Contemplation," in *Parochial and Plain Sermons* (London: Longmans, Green, 1908), II, 335–36.

59 See the letter of Newman to Mrs. John Mozley, January 19, 1837, in *The*

The French writer Ernest Psichari remarked on the same unhealthy symptom in the Hugenots. Mary Baker Eddy, the founder of the religion called Christian Science, describes it this way:

> I, I, I, I Itself, I.
> the inside and the outside, the what and the why;
> the when and the where, the will and the I;
> all I, I, I, I Itself, I.[60]

But Catholic mysticism is not of that sort at all. Our Lord said to St. Teresa: "Enclose thyself in Me, not Me in thyself." Although St. Paul warned Timothy to take heed to himself, he at the same time charges him to "be instant in season and out of season," in laboring for the welfare of his people (see 2 Tm 4:2). And St. Paul himself in the same letter boasts that he "endures all things for the sake of the elect" (see 2 Tm 2:10) and is content to be reckoned an evildoer if necessary to save their souls.

"Strip me of everything," St. Francis de Sales prayed, "only let me have souls." St. Cajetan was called the *Venator Animarum*—the Hunter of Souls. Do not say all your prayers for yourself, one of the saints advised; and St.

Letters and Diaries of John Henry Newman, Gerard Tracey, ed. (Oxford: Clarendon, 1984), VI, 16. The book about Wesley is Robert Southey, *The Life of Wesley; And the Rise and Progress of Methodism* (New York: Evert Duyckinck & George Long, 1820), 2 vols.

60 The words of the author's original quote were slightly incorrect and incorrectly attributed to the American poet Walt Whitman. The words actually come from the flyleaf of early versions of Mary Baker Eddy's *Science and Health: With Key to the Scriptures* (Boston: Christian Science Publishing, 1875). Eddy may have been unaware that the motto is based on a "burlesque" of Fichte's *Egoismus* offered by Samuel Taylor Coleridge in *Biographia Literaria* (Oxford: Clarendon Press, 1907), I, 101.

Teresa of Avila remarked: "I can't bear all this talking, talking about merit."

The saints had the hardihood to forgo applause and that public recognition without which philanthropic work, in our day, is considered to be hardly worth doing at all. In fact, they were often so ingenious in avoiding it that some of them were not appreciated in their lifetime. St. Vincent de Paul hated publicity and discouraged it in his followers. "A good work talked about," he used to say, "is a good work spoiled."

They did good by stealth often, and they literally blushed to find fame. St. Damien de Veuster, who gave his life ministering to lepers in Hawaii, never expected attention or admiration. Until his death, the world knew next to nothing of what he had been doing and suffering on his lonely island.

Apparently, he was not conscious that he had done anything extraordinary—had advanced beyond the line of ordinary moral obligation. It was simply his vocation, his job, just as it was Shakespeare's to write plays, or Marconi's to invent the radio. What could be more eloquent of the selfless simplicity of this priest than those words which he wrote to his friend Edward Clifford, shortly before the end: "My work, with all its faults and failures, is in [God's] hands, and before Easter I shall see my Savior."[61]

61 Edward Clifford, *Father Damien: A Journey From Cashmere to His Home in Hawaii* (London: Macmillan, 1889), 116.

SELFLESSNESS IN DYING

The saints were disengaged from self even in dying. How detached and dignified their deathbeds were!

When the Comte de Mirabeau, the French revolutionary, was drawing near to his end, he called loudly for opium. "You promised to spare me needless suffering," he said. They then gave him a cup of harmless liquid which he swallowed, believing it to be mortal.

Later he died, saying: "Support this head, the greatest head in France." This is the sort of stuff that the heroes of this world are made of.

Now contrast this with the deathbed of St. Louis, another Frenchman. His biographer tells us that when this king drew near to the end, he talked incessantly of Tunis in Africa, and of the great desire he had to see the gospel preached there.

Indeed, Mirabeau is put to shame even by a woman—a Frenchwoman. "If God hears my prayers, there will be no last words of mine to repeat, for I shall say nothing at all." This is what St. Madeleine Sophie Barat said shortly before her death, and sure enough, her prediction was verified because she had a stroke a few days before the end.

This most difficult of all forms of self-forgetfulness is strikingly exemplified in our own English martyrs. They certainly indulged in "last words" according to the custom of the time, but their last words were never selfish words. "Jesus convert England; Jesus have mercy on this country"—thus spoke Henry Heath, the Franciscan, when martyred at Tyburn in 1643.

At the same place in 1595, the Jesuit Robert Southwell had said: "For my most miserable country I pray the light of truth and that it may learn to seek its eternal good in the right way."

"For my part," said John Pibush in 1601, "I hope my death will do more good than ever my life would have done."

"If," said Thomas Reynolds forty years later, "I had as many lives as there are bright stars in the firmament, I would gladly give them all for this cause."

Before him, Edmund Arrowsmith declared that nothing grieved him so much as "this England which I pray God soon to convert."

And in 1641 we have this from Alban Roe: "When you see our heads fixed up over the bridge, think that they are there to preach to you the very same faith for which we are about to die."

THE ASCETICISM OF THE SAINTS

THE SAINT is never a mere ascetic. That is to say, he is never a merely negative person, refusing, limiting, abstaining, and stopping there. He is above all a positive person, a creator.[62]

He cuts off only so that he may add something better. He deprives himself for a purpose, just as the athlete deprives himself for a purpose. He empties the vessel out and then sets about recharging it with something else.

St. Peter gave up his fishing boat and net and in return gained the whole world. The temptations of St. Anthony are not the whole of St. Anthony, in spite of Flaubert.[63] St. Anthony was a very positive person.

Self-sacrifice does not mean self-destruction. It does not mean making oneself useless. It means making oneself holy and therefore more useful than ever. A gap

---

62 This paragraph seems to be a paraphrase of a few lines from Algar Thorold, "Introduction," in *The Book of the Divine Consolation of the Blessed Angela of Foligno*, trans. Mary G. Steegmann (London: Chatto & Windus, 1909), xxii.

63 The French author Gustave Flaubert spent much of his life writing a book entitled *La Tentation de Saint Antoine* (The Temptation of Saint Anthony).

is made, indeed, but it is presently filled by a new and greater interest or activity.

Humility, for example, if it destroys one energy, replaces it at once by another and a better energy. Humility is the opposite of timidity.

"Long ago," said Blessed Charles de Foucauld to a lady, "I found out how to be happy."

"How?" she asked.

"By abstaining from pleasure," was the answer.

For twenty-five years he never slept in a bed, and in his hermitage in the Sahara he slept on the step of the altar like a dog at the feet of its master. Yet he had to acknowledge that he had far more restful nights there than in his luxurious flat at Paris.

So true is it, as St. Bernard said, that the mortified man is able to suck honey from the rock and oil from the rugged stones. Such are the compensations of asceticism. It has a positive value.

ASCETICISM, THE PURIFIER

In the early ages of Christianity asceticism was the disinfectant that purified a society corrupted by pagan excess. To destroy the tyranny of desire, to become the master of one's appetites, to subdue the lower nature, to quiet the clamor of the flesh—and to do all these things in order that the soul may be free, may not be trampled upon by the body, may rise, may elevate itself and attain to the full stature of its dignity and nobility, and at length to its eternal dwelling place—this is the explanation of these fastings and these extreme renunciations. It was this that drove St. Mary into Egypt, St. Bavon into his hollow tree, and St. Simon to the top of his pillar.

St. Ammon, who became one of the most illustrious of the ancient Fathers of the Desert, on his marriage day read to his young bride the praises of virginity found in St. Paul's first epistle to the Corinthians (see 1 Cor 7:32–35). Inspired by the reading, she at once entered into an agreement with her husband to live as brother and sister. God certainly recompensed their heroic sacrifice.

For eighteen years they were happy together and made great strides in the ways of perfection, until by mutual consent they separated and went into solitude. She formed a community of religious women, and he became Abbot of Nitria. Twice a year, however, he visited his bride and consoled her with the assurance of an eternal reunion.

When the English art critic John Ruskin visited the Grande Chartreuse, the mother house of the Carthusian religious order perched in the French Alps, he went into ecstasies over the view. The monk said to him: "We do not come here to look at the scenery."

This is not just sourness or moroseness or being culpably blind to the color and sparkle of life. It is simply the exercise of a choice. We cannot look at two separate things at once, and the saint ignores the beauties of nature so that he may fix his gaze upon the beauties of grace.

When St. Thomas Aquinas walked along the banks of Lake Geneva, without noticing the lake, it meant only that the eyesight of his mind was riveted upon another and a better vision. After all, even earthly lovers are at certain moments blind to any light, save the light in one another's eyes.

St. Anthony of Padua in dying ignored everything and everyone, save the "Reward exceeding great" (Gn 15:1 Douay-Rheims) that awaited him. "I see God," he said, and so he died.

In his famous letter to Eustochium, St. Jerome tells how and why he came to abandon the study of the classical writers. It was a painful and heroic sacrifice for such a man of taste to make, but the man himself and indeed the whole Church was the gainer in the end. The saint wrote:

> Falling into a trance, I seemed to myself to be arraigned before the tribunal of Christ. Being asked my profession, I answered that I was a Christian. "You lie," said the judge; "you are a Ciceronian: for the works of Cicero possess your heart." . . . And from that time onward I gave myself to the reading of divine things with greater diligence and attention than I had ever read other authors.[64]

The saintly Benedictine bishop Charles Walmesley was Vicar Apostolic of the Midland District of England about the middle of the eighteenth century. It is related of him that he abandoned his favorite study, mathematics, owing to a distraction which he had while saying Mass. He was one of the greatest mathematicians of his time and was consulted regarding the revision of the calendar by the English government.

One morning during the Holy Sacrifice he noticed that the rays of the sun falling on the corporal had produced a sort of geometric pattern. Before he knew what

64 See his Letter 22, "To the Lady Eustochium," 30 (Rome, A.D. 394).

he was doing, he found himself setting to work to unravel a problem in trigonometry. Coming to his senses at last, he made in one and the same breath an apology to God and a resolution to have done with mathematics for ever. No one can deny that this was heroic, and no one can affirm that it was just a sterile relinquishment resulting only in a loss.

RENUNCIATION, A LAW OF THE GOSPEL

Certainly some of the saints carried the renunciation even of lawful things to very extreme lengths. This they did in the interests of the general principle of renunciation which, after all, is a law of the gospel. Principles are very important things to those who hold them, and what to the spectator appears very trivial is important by reason of the principle that inspires it.

There is the well-known story of the General of the religious order who was told by the doctor that one of his sick subjects ought to be sent to take the waters at a certain fashionable spa. "He will die otherwise," said the medical pundit.

"*Moriatur*," answered the General: "Let him die."

There are those whom this will shock. Yet nobody is shocked and most are edified when the English playwright George Bernard Shaw says: "If it is to be a question as to whether I am to die or the animals are to die for me to feed on, I accept death."

The Rule of St. Benedict counsels abstinence from laughter. The Benedictine monk is not forbidden to laugh. But on principle he is advised to laugh a little less than he feels inclined to do.

Newman defends St. Anthony the Hermit against the charge of fanaticism. His austerities were extreme, but he was never a morose man. His moderation and good sense shine out in all stories told about him. And as related by the ascetic writer John Cassian, Anthony himself insisted that discretion was the virtue most necessary for the attainment of perfection.

THE WORLD IS A TASK MASTER

The motive is everything after all. Allowing for the difference of motive, there is not a great deal to choose between the ascetic and the worldling. What can be more exhausting than the endless futilities of fashion and society? To have to live from day to day in an atmosphere of pretence, to have to canonize humbug, to study effect, to be occupied with form and appearance, to be debarred from saying what one really thinks—in short, to have to walk without moving the feet and to talk without moving the lips—this is asceticism of a very high, or rather low, order.

No monastic rule enforces its regulations so rigidly upon its members as does the world upon its devotees. The most detached and poverty-stricken saint could at any rate call his countenance his own—which is more than the slaves of appearances can do.

St. Lydwine of Schiedam and St. Rose of Lima made God a present of their good looks. There is some sense in a sacrifice of that sort, but none at all in immolating one's natural complexion upon the altar of cosmetics. There is probably far more discomfort involved in going with tortured feet to dance at midnight in a stuffy ballroom than there is in going with bare feet to pray at midnight in a peaceful convent chapel.

When Lord Perth, the Scottish earl, went to La Trappe Abbey to test his vocation, his uncle wrote to the abbot: "My nephew will never be content at La Trappe. He is very fastidious. He can never bear a bed soft enough, and the smallest wrinkle in the sheets keeps him awake all night." This is the penalty of self-indulgence.

St. Francis and the others who sold their goods and gave the money to the poor were really big men, much bigger men than those who have sold the poor and given the money to themselves. Detachment is really a mark of superiority and culture. "It is impossible," says Ruskin, "for an intellectually cultured man to make money the sole object of his life."

St. Juliana Falconieri is said never to have looked in a mirror. That requires courage, but it must require heroism to sit in front of a mirror for hours on end. The saints suffered and became strong, while the worldly suffer and become weak.

In one of his letters St. Leonard of Port Maurice has this passage: "We put ourselves to all sorts of inconveniences to satisfy our guilty passions. But when it is a question of overcoming them, we will not move a finger. It is just this halfpenny's worth of suffering that nobody wants to spend."

In other words, the saint is really economical with his hardships, and the worldling is prodigal. When the ancient Greek philosopher Socrates saw a rich man, he used to say, "There goes one more slave in golden chains." And the Scottish poet Thomas Campbell says:

Worth itself is but a charter
To be mankind's distinguished martyr.[65]

The saint gives up the love of creatures in exchange for the love of God. The worldling gives up the love of God and gets instead that insipid sort of hatred which in society passes for friendship. Blessed Henry Suso sums it all up when he says that worldly people often "purchase hell at a very dear price" by sacrificing themselves "to please the world."[66]

SACRIFICE LEADS TO PEACE AND FREEDOM

We cannot deny that by means of their independence of external things the saints attained to peace of mind and freedom of soul; and peace and freedom are real goods, desirable objects as even the worldly man will allow. In a multitude of possessions there is very little peace. Even the pagans noted that the master was usually the one slave of the household.

After all, contentment depends on how little one desires and how much one can put up with. If we advance a stage higher and consider the question of moral and spiritual improvement, then we must allow that the ascetics were on incontrovertible ground. The general weakening of Christian asceticism has only resulted in the general impoverishment of the spiritual life of Christians.

---

65 See Thomas Campbell, "A Dream," in *The Complete Poetical Works of Thomas Campbell*, J. Logie Robertson, ed. (repr., New York: Haskell House, 1968), 239.

66 See Blessed Henry Suso, *The Life of Blessed Henry Suso* (London: Burns, Lambert & Oates, 1865), 219.

"Without some portion of self-denial in all its forms, no great man ever attained to be good," wrote the Scottish philosopher Thomas Carlyle. Many sincere critics of religion, or rather of religious people, are saying that Christianity will never become the vital world force that it was unless and until Christians can bring themselves to accept the renunciations—even the extreme renunciations—that are inherent in their religion. Certainly those who flattered themselves that the removal of asceticism from religion would result in making it more popular have been sadly deceived.

The example of St. Anthony's asceticism kindled "a fire that many waters could not quench" (see Sg 8:6–7). The movement that he initiated contributed to the salvation of society, which in his day was rotted through with self-indulgence.

St. Peter Faber travelled on foot mostly, with the bundle of his writings tied round his neck. He made a vow never to accept any payment or compensation for his spiritual ministrations. Certainly his apostolate did not flourish the less by reason of this resolution.

"You see," said a great prelate to St. Thomas Aquinas, speaking of his wealth, "I cannot say with Peter, 'Silver and gold have I none.' "

"No," replied the saint, "and for that reason neither can you say with Peter, 'Arise, take up your bed and walk' " (see Acts 3:1–10).

THE ENERGY OF THE SAINTS

"STRONG reasons make strong actions." Here in a nutshell is the secret of the energy of the saints. A beehive is the emblem of many of them—of St. Bernard, for example—and it is not surprising.

"To occupy oneself with God," he used to say, "is not to be idle," and indeed he proved it. He would interrupt his sermons when the bell rang to announce the hour of manual labor, and he would say: "The priest ought always to be ready to exchange the chasuble for the plough." St. Francis de Sales wrote: "There is no labor where love is; or rather, the labor is sweet."

"A holy man was never yet an idle man": This truth is written clearly upon the records of saintliness. St. Francis Xavier and St. Vincent de Paul are striking evidences that sanctity never hinders activity. The life of the latter is an amazing succession of achievements and enterprises, and in the midst of it all he found time to write more than 30,000 letters—at any rate, 30,000 of his letters were extant in 1664.

The Spanish theologian Francisco Suárez had an ordinary working day of fifteen hours. Thomas à Kempis was one of the Brothers of the Common Life who were pledged to devote themselves to practical good works. Yet he was the author of a great number of books, *The Imitation of Christ* included. He was also an indefatigable copyist, and with his own hand wrote out the entire Bible, besides a large missal and many treatises of the Fathers of the Church.

The physician who attended St. John Bosco in his last illness said to the Salesian Fathers: "His malady can be traced to no direct cause. His life is simply worn out by work. He is not dying of any disease. He is like a lamp expiring for lack of oil."

It makes one feel tired only to read of the activities of St. Paul—only to think of him careering about Asia Minor and over the Mediterranean on those amazing journeys and voyages of his, debating, catechizing, preaching and, no doubt, in between getting on with his trade of making and mending tents! Truly, the breathless description of his toils and exertions, which he addressed to the Corinthians, was no exaggeration (see 2 Cor 11:23–33). And we must remember that his sermons were not just the sort of "lick and a promise" that we are used to nowadays.

The one which he preached at Troas lasted until midnight. This is a memorable occasion, in a way, because it is the earliest record we have of anyone daring to fall asleep during a Christian sermon. The culprit not only slept, but he fell out of the window during his nap and was found dead. St. Paul raised him to life; and then, says the Book of Acts, he "conversed with them a long while, until daybreak" (see Acts 20:7–12).

ASTONISHING ACHIEVEMENTS

The achievements of some of the saints fill us with astonishment. It puzzles us to come across those gigantic pieces of stone that defy the most powerful modern machinery, and which the ancients lifted about from place to place as though they were so many bundles of straw. In the same way, it fatigues the mind even to read about the work that some of the saints got through.

St. Alphonsus Liguori made a vow never to waste a moment of time, and he kept it. In the midst of all his other labors, St. Augustine contrived to write so much that the Benedictine edition of his works fills eleven enormous folio volumes. Yet these books were merely the by-products of an active episcopal life that would have absorbed the energy of several ordinary men.

St. Francis de Sales insisted again and again that besides loving God we must strive with all our might to render to our neighbor all the assistance that lies in our power. It was out of his sheer love for the faithful that St. Gregory abandoned his beloved monastery to take up what he called "the conflict of the papacy." It was never ambition that moved men such as St. Ambrose and St. Hugh of Lincoln to accept the responsibilities of high office, but their desire to do something for the Church at large.

"Do you accept your election?" the papal conclave asked Pius X.

"I accept it as a cross," was the answer.

St. Martin of Tours used to pray: "Lord, if I am necessary to your people, I will not shrink back from any toil."

St. Anthony preached his last Lenten course of sermons with a fatal illness upon him. One of the most beautiful accounts of a Christian deathbed is that of our own St. Bede, the medieval English priest-scholar. He died on the Vigil of the Ascension, and up to the very last he busied himself dictating a translation of the Gospel of St. John:

> In the evening the scribe Wilbert said to him: "There is still one sentence, dear master, which is not written down." And when this had been supplied and the boy had told him that it was finished, "You have spoken truth," Bede answered, "it is finished. Take my head in your hands so that sitting up, I may call upon my Father." And thus upon the floor of his cell, singing *Gloria Patri,* he peacefully breathed his last breath.[67]

"What is the secret of your success?" a lady once asked Turner the painter. "Work, madam, work," he answered. And the saints might say the same.

St. Isidore the farmer was devoted to prayer, but he was also devoted to his plough. When he was hard pressed for time, as farmers are apt to be, angels used to come and take charge of the plough while he prayed. But the point is that he never depended on the angels. Being a saint, he knew that God helps those who help themselves.

As another saint said: "We must labor as though everything depended on us, and we must pray as though everything depended on God." "What is worth doing is

---

67 From a letter on the death of St. Bede written by one of his disciples, the monk Cuthbert of Jarrow.

worth doing well," said one saint. "A great deal of talent is lost to the world for lack of a little energy," said another. St. Teresa said: "Teresa by herself can do nothing, but Teresa plus God can do everything." "Hell," said St. Jane Frances de Chantal, "is full of the talented—but heaven, of the energetic."

HOLINESS ENERGIZES

Holiness apparently energizes like nothing else. Grace vitalizes the very body so that there can be wrung from it the uttermost drop of service. St. Augustine, as we saw elsewhere, had a great penchant for puns. Here is his pun on the name of St. Firmus. "He was Firm by name, and grace made him Firmer."

The saints, wrote the English poet Francis Thompson, "scarce know the meaning of decrepitude."[68] An unspiritual condition exhausts the springs of our vitality. Self-gratification and excess devour the sinews of mind and body. Inordinate desires and appetites involve a riotous and deadly expenditure of energy and will; and on the other hand, "to subdue self is the secret of strength."

"If I could be born again," said St. Francis de Sales, "I would have fewer desires." We hear a great deal in our day about the dangers of what are called "repressions." But it is always by means of a prudent repression of impulses and feelings that the energies "condense within [the] soul and change to purpose strong."[69]

---

68 Francis Thompson, "Health and Holiness," in *The Works of Francis Thompson*, vol. 3, *Prose* (London: Burns, Gates and Washbourne), 279.

69 Newman, "Flowers Without Fruit," in *Verses on Various Occasions* (London: Longmans, Green, 1890), 169

A truly spiritual life imparts a unique sort of intensity to the will, an energy very different from the coarse and irresponsible kind of vibrations that are produced by stimulants or by eating quantities of animal food. A widespread and organized fallacy lurks behind the usual talk that goes on about "keeping up our strength." There is a recognized strength that is not worth keeping up, and if it were kept down instead of up, there would be less vice and less crime in the world.

But the energy of sanctity is a calm, a rational, and a responsible thing. It never loses its head.

St. Vincent de Paul was one of the most energetic men of modern times. He carried a daily and yearly burden of interests and commitments that would harass the average man and bathe him in a lather of perspiration. But St. Vincent was habitually cool and calm and collected, and those who interviewed him for the first time gathered the impression that he led a sheltered and tranquil life.

St. Catherine of Siena and St. Teresa of Ávila were workers, organizers. No "scorcher" or "hustler" among the busy women of modern times could survive for a week the labors and anxieties that these two sustained for a lifetime. But there was nothing "hot and bothered" about either St. Catherine or St. Teresa. "She is so restful," people said of the former, although as a matter of fact she was one of those whose days are passed on the edge of a volcano.

The same was remarked of St. Madeleine Sophie, that energetic genius who used to say: "A woman cannot remain neutral in this world. She too is set for the fall or the resurrection of many" (see Lk 2:34).

St. John Vianney, the Curé of Ars, ate next to nothing. He tried to live on grass, and in the end, he almost lived on potatoes and bread. He simply walked past all our fallacious expedients for "keeping up the strength." Yet judged by his output of exertion, the Curé of Ars was one of the strongest of men.

HOLINESS, THE SOURCE OF FORTITUDE

"It only needs an 'I will' to make us all God's," St. Margaret Mary said. And once we are all God's, we become all will, so that whatever our hands find to do, we do it with all our might. "Cast yourself," said St. Philip Neri, "into the arms of God, and be very sure of this: that if He wants anything of you, He will fit you for the work and give you strength."

It is never God's way to call His servants to a great contest without putting suitable weapons in their hands. Holiness is a perennial source of courage and fortitude. Souls formed by God cannot but be strong souls because He is the *Deus Fortis,* the Mighty God.

St. Francis of Assisi had a strength out of all proportion to the seeming frailty of his body. St. Gregory the Great is surely one of the most energetic figures in history, and yet he was never what we would call a strong man. He had a delicate appearance, and many of his stupendous enterprises were directed and controlled from a sickbed.

In the monks of the olden times—that is to say, in those very men who have been calumniated by a world that has made the laziness of the monk proverbial—we see a devouring activity. "To work is to pray" was the watchword of those primitive religious workers. When the monastic system was at its zenith, the one thing that it never produced was feebleness or enervation of character.

What it did produce was the *Athletae Christi*—the Athletes of Christ, men armed with a robust and vigorous personality. And it is striking that as soon as sanctity declined, energy declined with it. As soon as the monk began to talk about the changed times and the need of "keeping up his strength," his strength seemed to fail.

St. Bernard was a vegetarian. Yet the fire and vitality of St. Bernard were such that his sermons roused not just a chapel-full of devout worshippers, but a whole continent, sending good and bad men alike marching off to the Crusades.

The closing centuries of the medieval period stand out as the golden, the heroic, age of Christian activity. They were that because they were intensely spiritual. Creative work that is really worthwhile proceeds from the energy, not of the body and nerves, but of the spirit.

The thirteenth century boils over with energy. There was about it a fiery glow, and this fiery glow was fanned into flapping flame by the wind of the spirit. One of the greatest disasters that has overtaken the modern world is just this: It has lost its consciousness of the intimate connection between the soul and the body of man.

Bodies today are out of order largely because souls are out of order. The practice of medicine has become far too scientific, with a result that is obvious to all thoughtful people. Medicine has almost ceased to be a ministry of healing and has become instead a mere system of patch-work and superficial renovation.

THE WORK OF PEN AND INK

It is true that some of the saints were mainly saints of the pen and ink, but they were nonetheless real workers. To be nailed to a desk for days and weeks on end is one of the severest tests of the spirit of industry, and it is a test that few even industrious people could stand. The industry of bustle and movement is an easy thing in comparison with the industry that can submit to being confined and imprisoned.

St. Thomas's *Summa* represents a gigantic piece of real, hard work. St. Alphonsus stuck to his writing table until eyes and fingers refused their office. St. Theodosius wrote by hand the whole of the Bible without making a single blot.

It is all very well to talk about the delights of authorship and scholarship, but authors and scholars themselves are seldom consulted as to the other side of the picture. St. Jerome, however, whom some regard as the greatest of Latin Fathers, is quite frank on the subject of the sufferings which his own studies involved.

"What labor it cost me, what difficulties I went through, how often I despaired and left off, and how I began to learn again, both I who felt the burden can witness and they also who lived with me." However, he does add: "I thank Our Lord that I now gather sweet fruit from the bitter seed of those studies."

St. Augustine had the same arduous struggle to encounter. Clean contrary to what we might have expected, he tells us in his *Confessions:* "As a boy I did not love study and had to be forced into it."[70]

Energy, we know, is not enough without an opportunity. But it is very instructive to see how a sudden opportunity revealed unexpected energies and capabilities in the saints. We are largely indebted to the Great Fire of London for the monuments of Christopher Wren's genius; and in the same way, mere accident or chance often brought to light astonishing powers in God's servants.

What exactly did Christendom expect when Gregory I was elected pope? We do not know, but we do know what it got. Here was a quiet and peaceful man of prayer, a cloistered and therefore narrow and timid soul as men, no doubt, imagined.

This recluse, however, was not destined to die in his happy valley of obscurity. The hour came, and a great man was needed. The monk with the downcast eyes ascended the papal chair and proceeded to astonish Europe.

Examples of this sort of thing might be multiplied almost indefinitely. In the moment of crisis some saint steps through a door in the wall that no one had noticed and, unannounced and unheralded, he makes his way to the front. And because he is a saint, he sets the place on fire. St. Teresa was no doubt thinking of this very thing when she said so candidly: "If I had been a man, I would have been a great preacher."

---

70 See Augustine, *Confessions*, I, 12, 19.

THE DETACHMENT OF THE SAINTS

"HE WHO wishes to dwell in his inmost interior must rid himself of all multiplicity" is the advice given by Blessed Henry Suso. It is a very sane and commonsense piece of advice. But to carry it out, we need to be detached. Again he says: "A detached man . . . should be always looking to see what he can do without."[71]

This looking about to see what we can do without would contribute enormously to our total wellbeing, physical and spiritual, had we but the courage to apply ourselves to it. Suso is very emphatic on the management of our external affairs with a view to our inner development. "Give heed also," he says, "to your outward man, that it be one with your inward man."[72]

The saints well understood the connection between the outward and the inward. By liberating themselves from all unnecessary attachments, they were striking a most decisive blow in defense of their spiritual freedom. The sacrifice of wealth and luxury that is so uniform a feature of Catholic sanctity has this very practical purpose.

71 Suso, 267, 277.

72 See Suso, 279.

THE BAGGAGE OF RICHES

"Riches are to virtue what baggage is to an army"—this is the saying of Sir Francis Bacon, an English philosopher who was not a Catholic at all. Even the pagan philosophers were well aware of the blight that almost inevitably accompanies the possession of wealth. According to them, the rich man is condemned to live with his head bowed down to the earth.

But the saints were not at all anxious to live with their heads bowed down to the earth. They were bent upon walking erect and on looking upwards as the human being is plainly intended to do. They were intent upon breathing the free air of heaven—and according to the Gospel, the wealthy find it difficult to breathe at all. "They are choked by the riches of life" (see Lk 8:14).

"If you would rise," said St. John Chrysostom, "shun luxury, for luxury lowers and degrades." "Elevation of character is never to be found among the luxurious," said St. Augustine. And, indeed, in the obscurity and poverty of the slums you may witness a magnanimity and nobility beyond the credence of the worldly—spectacles of moral strength and endurance to which the pampered and the fashionable are perfect strangers.

"Luxury is cowardly, and it is cruel," St. Jerome wrote. And as human beings we may well rejoice at the thought of those who by renouncing the cowardice of luxury avoided its cruelty.

> Thank God for poverty
> That makes and keeps us free,
> That lets us go our unobtrusive way,

Glad of the sun and rain,
Upright, serene, humane,
Contented with the fortune of a day.[73]

The man who wrote these lines was not a saint, but the saints one and all would have endorsed the truth of every line of it. St. Francis reprobated money and kicked it right out of his way, with the result that he attained to a splendid degree of spiritual liberty, was "glad of the sun and rain and contented with the fortune of the day" as few lovers of nature ever have been. They evidently well knew what they were doing, these saints.

St. Fabiola, as she drew near to death, gave away her remaining possessions in order, as she said, to lighten her soul for its journey to paradise. "Alas!" said the dying St. Paul of the Cross, "I have nothing to bequeath to you but my bad example."

When St. John Bosco was in the last extremity, he said to the Father who stood by his bed: "Take my pocketbook and purse out of my soutane, and if there is any money in them send it to Don Rua. I want to die so poor that they may say: Don Bosco died without leaving a halfpenny." Evidently Don Bosco could see nothing very edifying in the wills of religious people.

When St. Agnes of Bohemia, the Poor Clare, was dying she bequeathed as a legacy to her daughters this piece of advice: "Hold fast to poverty: It is the blood and life of our religion." So, too, when St. Lawrence O'Toole was asked on his deathbed if he had made his will, he

73 [William] Bliss Carman, "The Word at St. Kavin's," in *Pipes of Pan*, vol. 4, *Songs From a Northern Garden* (Boston: L. C. Page, 1904), 87.

said: "What are you talking about? Thank God I haven't a penny left in the world."

St. Angela Merici's will consisted of thirteen spiritual clauses, each containing a legacy of good advice. Pope St. Gregory VII had nothing to bequeath except his episcopal insignia, his mitre going to St. Anselm of Lucca. Here is St. Athanasius' account of the last testament of St. Anthony the Hermit:

> Distribute my garments as follows: Let Athanasius the bishop have the one sheepskin and the garment I sleep on which he gave me new and which has grown old with me. Let Serapion, the bishop, have the other sheepskin. As to my hair shirt, keep it for yourselves. And now, my children, farewell! Anthony is going and is no longer with you.[74]

THE LESSON OUR GENERATION NEEDS

"We are poor and must live as poor people," St. Paul of the Cross used to say to his brethren. It happened once that he was summoned to an audience with the Pope at a time when his congregation was in desperate straits for lack of money. He was accompanied by the rector of one of his houses, who naturally hoped and expected that the Holy Father would give them generous alms.

At the end of the interview, as they were taking their leave, the Pope asked: "Are you in lack of anything?"

To the horror of the rector, St. Paul answered: "No, we are only too well off."

74 See St. Athanasius, *The Life and Affairs of Our Holy Father Anthony*, 91.

By thus stripping money of its social importance, the saints have conferred an immense boon upon society. Their renunciation and voluntary poverty is perhaps the lesson that our generation needs most of all. At the moment, Mammon towers above us like the ugly and relentless pagan idol that it is, and unfortunately, there are nominal Christians who are bowing and scraping at its feet.

"It is certain," says the American philosopher and psychologist William James, "that the prevalent fear of poverty among the educated classes is the worst moral disease from which our civilization suffers." And he adds: "Among us English-speaking peoples especially do the praises of poverty need once more to be boldly sung."[75]

But we require more, and much more, than the mere singing of poverty's praises. Some of the pagans sang the praises of poverty in very rapturous strains, but the rapturous strains did not always succeed in converting the singers themselves. In ancient Rome, the Stoic philosopher Seneca and the historian Sallust wrote well of detachment while at the same time being noted for their rapacity and avarice.

Indeed, the grand deficiency of pagan philosophy was its practical deficiency. Nobody seemed able to get the thing to work. Individuals saw the light, but they had not energy enough to reach it.

---

75 William James, "The Value of Saintliness," Lectures 14 and 15 in *The Varieties of Religious Experience*, in *William James: Writings 1902–1910* (New York: Library of America, 1987), 334, 333.

"I see the better path," Ovid, one of their poets, admitted, "and I approve it. But I continue to follow the baser path."[76] It was in fact reserved to Christianity to bridge the deep gulf that lay between promise and performance, theory and practice.

St. Francis sang the praises of poverty, but he did more—and it was because he did this "more" that his singing did not sound falsetto. The greed and avarice of society will not be challenged by mere poets, but by asceticism, by those who are lifted clean above the grasping crowd like the Curé of Ars. The men who really counted in antiquity were poor men. The great reformers who changed the direction of thought in any country have all lived on very little.

THE POWER OF DETACHMENT

St. Philip Neri maintained that detachment is the source of all spiritual power. He went farther and asserted that if he could lay hold of a dozen really detached men, he would guarantee to convert the world. St. Ignatius Loyola went very far toward proving that this is so. "Do the impossible for Me, and I will do it for you"—this is what Our Lord seemed to say to Blessed Charles de Foucauld, the Hermit of the Sahara.

"The great and decisive stroke which will reform the world," says a modern writer, "if it ever comes, will be initiated by one of those beings who have made the great sacrifice, by one of those who have the right to command

---

76 See Ovid, *Metamorphoses* VII, 20: "*Video meliora, proboque, deteriora sequor.*"

men's hearts because they have bruised their own, by one of those whose brow is marked by the triple vow of obedience, poverty, and chastity."

The world refuses to be influenced by ordinary people and by any except very uncommon means. It exacts very great sacrifices from those who would hope to do anything good for it. Only the irreproachable have real moral influence.

The Passionist Father Ignatius Spencer belonged to a noble family. He was asked once why he travelled third class, and he answered: "Because there is no fourth." His superior, the venerable Father Dominic, when he went on his mission carried the day's food with him in the form of a couple of dried herrings. It is no wonder that these men were instrumental in effecting many remarkable conversions.

While still an Anglican, Newman penned the following lines:

> The unstable multitude cannot be influenced . . . except by uncommon means, by the evident sight of disinterested and self-denying love, and elevated firmness. . . . Heathens, and quasi-heathens . . . were not converted in the beginning of the Gospel, nor now . . . by the sight of domestic virtues or domestic comforts in their missionary.[77]

Perhaps in these latter days we have become too worldly-wise and have exaggerated the importance of money. When St. Alphonsus took possession of his

77 Newman, *Discussions and Arguments on Various Subjects* (London: Longmans, Green, 1899), 12.

episcopal see, he found himself in great straits. "Here we are," he said cheerfully, "an old bishop, an old coachman, an old carriage, and a pair of old horses." But the straits and the old carriage and horses did not prevent him from doing wonders.

"When God sees us too intent on worldly ways and means," said St. Teresa, "He just leaves us to ourselves." "As having nothing," said St. Paul, "and yet possessing everything" (see 2 Cor 6:10). St. Cajetan made a vow to depend on Providence without ever asking or planning, and Providence never let him down.

THE TRUE TEST OF DETACHMENT

The Church has set a grand and inspiring example of detachment from those ways and means that seem so necessary to us. We must judge the Church not by what she happens to possess, but by her behavior when her possessions are taken from her. This is the true test of detachment.

"A man's poverty before God," says St. Augustine, "is judged by the dispositions of his heart and not by his coffers." The Church has never sulked over her losses nor wasted valuable time in self-pity and regrets.

At the Wailing Wall in Jerusalem, this is the sorrowful liturgy that one hears.

> *The Rabbi:* For our temple that is destroyed
> *The People:* We sit solitary and weep.
> *The Rabbi:* For our majesty that is passed
> *The People:* We sit solitary and weep.[78]

---

78 See Pierre Loti, *Jerusalem and the Holy Land*, W. P. Baines, trans. (Philadelphia: David McKay, 1920), 118.

But the Church does not exhaust her energies in useless lamentations over this or that piece of vanished pomp or splendor. She has proved to the world again and again that she can part with her possessions and with her splendors without turning aside from her appointed tasks.

Cardinal Newman did not hesitate to place detachment among the notes of the Church. It is, he wrote, "one of the special ecclesiastical virtues of the popes. They are of all men exposed to the temptation of secular connections; and as history tells us, they have been of all men least subject to it. . . . [A conservative in religion] means a man who defends religion not for religion's sake, but for the sake of its accidents and externals; and in this sense conservative a pope can never be."[79]

Pope St. Gregory VII, the renowned Hildebrand, went penniless into exile, and Abbot Desiderius of Monte Cassino had to send him money for his needs while on the road. His death soon after "moved to tears all religious men and women, but especially the poor." When Pope Pius IX was driven out of Rome, it only amused him to find that he had come away with only a few coppers in his purse.

Pope St. Pius X reduced his personal expenses to a mere shadow. He dismissed the chefs: "What are they for?" he asked. "Seven chefs to prepare a little soup and two eggs!" He practically lived on rice and peas, which he wanted his sisters to cook for him so that he could dismiss the kitchen staff. It was reckoned that he lived on five francs a day.

79 Newman, *Rise and Progress of Universities*, 131–33.

When the Archbishop of New York, John McCloskey, was made America's first Cardinal, a group of his well-to-do countrymen presented him with a gorgeous carriage lacquered in scarlet and gold, and lined with crimson satin. The Cardinal hardly knew whether to laugh or to cry when the gift arrived. "He took one ride in it to the amazement of the town and the hoots of the newsboys, got out, and came home in a cab."

Addressing the spoliators of the Church, a modern writer says: "Very well! Take the gold pectoral crosses from our bishops! What will they do? They will wear crosses of wood instead, remembering that it was by means of a cross of wood that the world was saved."

St. Alphonsus pawned his pectoral cross in order to relieve the poor. He kept his ring only because the pawnbrokers would give him nothing for it. When the Redemptorist Father Hugh Macdonald was made bishop of Aberdeen, he continued to sleep on straw, he never drove if he could possibly walk, and his pectoral cross was made of aluminum.

"This is the rock upon which everyone splits today," said Lacordaire. "People no longer know how to live on little."[80] But in the very highest ranks of the Church there have always been multitudes who knew how to live on little.

The shoes that St. Alphonsus had to wear as a bishop lasted him for twenty-five years. The ring that the Duchess of Piedmont presented to St. Francis de Sales spent

80 Montalembert, *Memoir of the Abbé Lacordaire* (London: Richard Bentley, 1863), 188.

its time in going and returning from the pawnshop. The only present that St. Ignatius could make to St. Francis Xavier when the latter set out for the Indies was his own waistcoat.

When Pope Pius IX was Bishop of Spoleto, he wished to send some money to relieve the distress of the Irish famine. However, he had no money to send and only scraped together the £4 that he forwarded to the Bishop of Kerry by selling his silver plate. Father Dominic the Passionist scraped together his contribution to the victims of the same famine by making his community do without some of the food allowed by their rule.

THE CUSTODY OF THE EYES

Some of the saints excelled in a form of detachment that certainly can do us no harm: the custody of the eyes. It may hurt not to eat, but it can never hurt not to look. St. Alphonsus used to say that he who cannot bridle his curiosity is a lost man.

St. Hugh of Lincoln never knew the color of the horse on which he made the visitations of his diocese. St. John Neumann, the bishop of Philadelphia, passed close to Niagara Falls and refused to turn aside to see them.

St. Peter of Alcántara lived for three years in a house of his order without knowing any of the friars except by their voice. He worshipped and prayed in the same church for years without ever knowing that its roof was vaulted; and he went in and out of the convent without noticing the tree that grew at its door. He ate constantly in the same refectory without seeing anything of it except the little bit of the table at which he sat.

For a time, it was his duty to provide the food for the refectory. The superior reprimanded him because for six months he had given the brothers no dried fruit. The saint answered that he had never seen any dried fruit around. This was perfectly true, because although it was hanging from the ceiling of the kitchen where he worked, he had never noticed it. "He told me," says St. Teresa of Ávila, "that even after years he did not know his way about the neighborhood of the friary unless he followed the other friars."

The prior of Cluny once set St. Bernard off riding on a richly caparisoned horse. When he halted at the Grande Chartreuse monastery, the Carthusians were greatly shocked until they perceived that Bernard had been quite unaware of the luxurious style in which he had been travelling. After all, this is only a rather extreme and literal rendering of the Gospel text about plucking out the eye if it gives us scandal (see Mt 5:29).

Some busybody told St. Francis de Sales that a certain devout lady penitent of his actually wore fashionable earrings. "Does she indeed?" he answered. "Well, I was not aware that she had ears, much less earrings."

It was remarked of the late Cardinal Vaughan that when he administered Confirmation, he never looked at the godmother. This was just a mortification that the saintly prelate imposed upon his eyes. It implied neither a slight nor an insinuation, for we may be quite sure that some of the godmothers were well worth looking at.

THE HEROISM OF THE SAINTS

THE SAINTS were all heroes. Therefore they were in the good sense extremists and enthusiasts, because cold calculation never yet made a hero.

"It is . . . the intense conviction," writes Newman, "the indomitable resolve . . . the momentary crisis . . . the concentrated energy . . . which is the instrument of heaven."[81] A great danger lurks in our worship of the ordinary. There are far too many ordinary people in the world. It is the ordinary person who contributes most to the cheapening and degrading of life.

But no real Christian has a right to be ordinary. "You did not choose Me," Our Lord says, "but I chose you" (Jn 15:16). This means that something really distinctive and extra must characterize the selection, the choice, of Jesus Christ. In his letter to Titus, St. Paul insists that there must be something peculiar or special, something different about the Christian (see Ti 2:7).

The saints, of course, are just the pick of the whole

81 Newman, "Duties of Catholics Toward the Protestant View," Lecture 9 in *Lectures on the Present Position of Catholics in England* (London: Longmans, Green, 1908), 389–90.

basket, the flowers of the flock. They were men and women of real elevation of character, lifted clean above the humdrum and the average. Certainly the saints shunned peculiarity, and they had a horror of what religious call "exceptions." But at the same time they refused to walk the mediocre path.

"Sanctity," said St. Francis de Sales, "does not consist in being odd, but it does consist in being rare." St. John of the Cross asked two favors from God: first, that he might not die a prelate; second, that he might die in a place where he was unknown. In other words, St. John of the Cross was a very rare and unusual sort of person.

The saints were all specialists. St. Aloysius made a motto of the text *Age quod agis*. This may be translated in various ways, such as "Do [well] what you are doing." But it implies a kind of high temperature that "goes at" a thing instead of just going through with it—the ardor that carries everything before it.

NO MEDIOCRITY IN SANCTITY

The saints did not disdain the beaten track of spirituality in the sense that they planned it on original lines. But they certainly disdained the average or mediocre level of the Christian life. Most of them seemed to have had a great partiality for living dangerously.

They resemble those sea birds that are not really happy, do not really live, except when the tempest is at its height. In calm weather they seem to decline and dwindle; they are unable to content themselves upon a peaceful shore. They rise with the occasion and are strengthened by opposition and trial.

St. Athanasius was such a saint, and so was St. Gregory the Great. So most emphatically was St. Paul.

St. Alonzo Rodriguez always insisted that "at least three times a week" means four times a week. The average Christian may think this silly, and he may be able to support his view with any amount of casuistry.[82] But the ascetics never relied upon casuistry because they knew, what indeed is the fact, that casuistry is not and was never meant to be a rule of conduct.

Casuistry is a great and very necessary science, but it has dangers of its own. "A man," says the Abbé Henri Huvelin, "who spends his whole life compiling cases of conscience is not living in a healthy atmosphere." Casuistry as a rule of life will end by "trying to find the pleasures of hell in the arms of God."

We come across those who are enthusiasts for chess, for heraldry, for stamp-collecting, and so on. But the saints were simply enthusiastic about God. They were inspired all the time by an exceptional love, and they acted accordingly.

The *Mirror of Perfection* describes St. Francis as being drunk with love and compassion. Blessed Sebastian Valpre used to say that he who really loves God never uses the word enough; and the saintly author of the medieval

82 We must note here, in addition to the common contemporary meaning of *casuistry* as "specious argumentation or rationalization," the word's traditional theological meaning: "Casuistry is the science of applied moral theology. From the general principles of morality the casuist determines what one ought to do in given circumstances and the innocence or amount of guilt to be attached to a given act." *A Catholic Dictionary*, Donald Attwater, ed. (repr., Charlotte, N.C.: TAN Books, 2010), 78–79.

Ancren Rule for solitary religious tells the sisters: "Love makes all things easy. What do men and women not endure for a false love, and would endure more?"

The very pagans recognized this. "To the lover," said Cicero, "nothing seems excessive." St. Lydwine always insisted that the certain antidote to suffering is love. And certainly nobody would think much of a love that was never extravagant, was always sober, cool, and measured, and prided itself on avoiding extremes.

Toward the end of his life, St. John of the Cross was given the choice of two monasteries in which to pass the rest of his days in peace and quiet. Although he suffered severely at the hands of the authorities, he yet deliberately chose the monastery that was governed by a superior extremely hostile to himself. That is to say, true to his habit, he chose the path of heroism and not what we sometimes call the "sensible" path.

SANCTITY AND SELF-MASTERY

It is a fact as interesting as it is undeniable that mankind in general does award the chief place in its esteem for those saints who went to the greatest extremes. The lives of the ancient Fathers of the Desert have never ceased to fascinate and probably never will. Of the acts of the martyrs, the Calvinist Joseph Scaliger wrote: "I with truth aver, that there is nothing in the whole history of the Church with which I am so much moved: When I read them, I seem no longer to possess myself."[83]

83 As quoted in Butler, I, vi.

Non-Catholic scholars, when they interest themselves in the saints at all, are found concentrating upon the ascetics, the contemplatives, and the ecstatics. In his introduction to the English translation of the *Book of Divine Consolation of the Blessed Angela of Foligno*, Algar Thorold attempts an explanation of this attitude.[84]

He says that the heroism of the saint represents an achievement to which all men instinctively aspire. This achievement is the wielding of power, power over the circumstances of life and the blind forces of nature, and above all power over themselves, over their own passions and appetites. Man has in him the instinct of conquest, and indeed since the Fall conquest is man's supreme mission in life. But the heroic sort of saint exemplifies this instinct of conquest rising to the highest point it can reach, namely, self-mastery.

A complete victory gained over the senses and appetites represents to the ordinary human being the very summit of self-control. He is not prepared perhaps to emulate it, but he respects it in his heart. He admires it as he admires the exercise of all feats of strength.

The fascination of history largely arises from the admiration we feel for big-scale power. Heroic sanctity does require character; and character commands greater admiration than even genius.

It is true that the unbeliever views the saint solely in the light of an interesting study. He does not "believe" in him in the way in which the devout do. His interest in sanctity is a psychological interest pure and simple. But

---

84 See Thorold, xx–xxi.

all the same he is interested, and he is interested mainly in its most elevated and most heroic products.

It was St. Mary of Egypt, that most amazing of all the amazing anchorites, that the French historian Ernest Renan declared he would have given everything he possessed to have seen. The French writer Émile Zola, like Renan, had no use for theology and not a great deal of use for virtue. But when he came face to face with the heroism of the martyrs, he could not help himself; he simply had to let himself go.

> The executioners expose to the flies the martyrs whose bodies are covered with honey; they make them walk with bare feet over broken glass or red-hot coals, put them in ditches with reptiles; chastise them with whips, whose thongs are weighted with leaden balls; nail them when alive in coffins, which they throw into the sea; hang them by their hair, and then set fire to them; moisten their wounds with quicklime, boiling pitch, or molten lead; make them sit on red-hot iron stools; burn their sides with torches; break their bones on wheels, and torture them in every conceivable way. And with all this, physical pain counts for nothing. . . . Sebastian smiles, although pierced with arrows. . . . Molten lead is swallowed as if it were ice water. . . . The gridiron of St. Lawrence is of an agreeable freshness to him. . . . Cecilia, placed in a boiling bath, is refreshed by it. Christina exhorts those who would torture her. . . . [St. Vincent's] limbs are broken . . . he is pricked with needles, he is placed on a

> brazier of live coals, and then taken back to prison . . . a great light fills his dungeon, and angels sing with him, giving him rest as if he were on a bed of roses.[85]

We must be grateful, profoundly grateful, for everything that is extreme in the lives of God's servants. "The inimitable things in the saints," said St. Teresa, "often do us the most good." We are not thinking merely of that uneasy yet pleasurable sensation of wading deeper and deeper in the tide of life that their stupendous heroism provides, but of something much more important. A general absence of heroism would constitute a serious problem for Christianity.

Our critics are very fond of saying that in the interests of the average and ordinary Christian our religion has been shorn of its outstanding qualities. They say it has been so accommodated that it has lost its power to inspire. They judge our religion entirely by its lower and even lowest levels, and naturally conclude that little in the way of uplift is to be looked for in our quarter.

This is, of course, just one-sidedness and superficiality—a failure to realize that there are other levels besides what is called "the bourgeois level." Heroic sanctity has never failed in the Church—not for a single day. The supply of ardent, generous, and exceptional Christians is inexhaustible.

---

85 Émile Zola, *The Dream*, Eliza E. Chase, trans. (London: Chatto & Windus, 1907), 30–31.

HEROISM AND PERSECUTION

At the end of his study of St. Anthony the Hermit, Newman writes: "If I must choose between the fashionable doctrines of one age and of another, certainly I shall prefer that which requires self-denial, and creates hardihood and contempt of the world, [over] some of the creeds now in esteem, which rob faith of all its substance, its grace, its nobleness, and its strength, and excuse self-indulgence by the arguments of spiritual pride, self-confidence, and security."[86]

It is perhaps for this reason that God subjects the Church to continuous persecution. The English Catholic convert Father Frederick Faber maintained that the Church is less at home in the concordat than in the catacomb. And even *The Cambridge Modern History* acknowledges that the Church won back her power through her ability to suffer.

St. Jerome was quite emphatic on the value of these terrible trials. "You are deceived," he says, "if you think that a Christian can live without persecution. He suffers the greatest [persecution] who lives under none. Nothing is more to be feared than too long a peace. A storm puts a man upon his guard, and obliges him to exert his utmost efforts to escape shipwreck."[87]

St. Jane Frances de Chantal stepped over the prostrate body of her own son in order to enter religion. It is unfair to say that this is just unnatural. It *is* unnatural, but

86 Newman, *The Church of the Fathers* (London: J. G. F. & J. Rivington, 1840), 382.

87 As quoted in Butler, IX, 344.

it is also supernatural. It is a generous victory gained over the strongest instinct of a woman's heart.

The trouble with the world is that it allows its aversion to spirituality to distort its judgment. If sacrifices of this sort were made for a motive that the world really appreciates, they would be acclaimed as courageous and sensational deeds. We shall understand this if we take two parallel cases, the first belonging to the history of science and the other to the history of the Church.

François Huber, one of the masters of apiarian science, was born in 1750 and fell blind in his earliest youth. Thirty-nine years later he published the first volume of his *Observations on Bees*—a treasure house into which every subsequent writer on the subject has dipped. This man, in fact, became passionately absorbed in his researches and yet never with his own eyes did he behold a comb of honey.

To the veil in which nature enwraps her secrets was added the veil on his own dead eyes. Huber depended upon the assistance of his faithful servant Burnens, guiding with his intelligence the eyes and the hands of the other who had the real vision. It has, indeed, been said that in the annals of human suffering and human triumph, there is nothing more poignant and no lesson more admirable than the story of this patient collaboration and this victory over one of the heaviest forms of physical defeat.

We shall not quarrel with this. Science has a perfect right to be proud of Huber; but we may be permitted to compare his achievement with that of the famous director of the catechetical school of Alexandria, the saintly

Didymus. St. Jerome tells us that this man lost his sight in infancy when he was just beginning to learn the alphabet.

Later he had letters cut in wood and learned to distinguish them by the touch. With the help of readers and scribes he mastered almost all the sacred and profane authors and acquired a thorough knowledge of grammar, rhetoric, logic, arithmetic, music, geometry, astronomy, the philosophy of Plato and Aristotle, and particularly the Holy Scriptures. At the same time he was a man of prayer and of piety—probably the most accomplished blind man who ever lived. Even better than Huber he proved that no affliction or infirmity need warrant our abandoning the search after light and truth.

EVERYDAY HEROISM

We can all recognize the heroism of such examples, but what we do not appreciate so easily is the genuine heroism that may underlie the life that is externally commonplace and unexciting. And yet the grandiose and dramatic situation is not always the severest test to which virtue can be put. Dramatic situations can be very stimulating. There is a certain ecstasy and exaltation that accompanies even the ordeal of martyrdom, so that in a very real sense it may demand nearly as much courage to live for the faith as to die for it.

The eighteenth century tested English Catholics severely. The force of active and direct persecution was spent. The rack and the gibbet had been put away. There were few fines and confiscations.

But at the same time there was something that proved even harder to endure. There was a cold-blooded, unromantic sort of isolation and repression. This was the period of some very serious apostasies. The descendants of those who had braved dungeon, fire, and sword conformed at a time of comparative peace, simply because they could not endure their exclusion from office and from the public life of the nation.

Cardinal Gasquet strongly emphasizes the importance of this period as the real testing time of English Catholicism. He bids us admire the heroism of that rapidly dwindling band enduring for the faith of their fathers something almost worse than torture and death. There is martyrdom and there is martyrdom.

"God's will be done today and tomorrow and forever without an 'if' or a 'but.'" This aspiration of St. Jane Frances de Chantal might easily involve very real heroism. The world allows itself to be dazzled by the pillar of St. Simon Stylites, but never reflects upon the secret heroism of the vows of the religious life—the heroism of monotony, the heroism that gets no recognition or applause from men and seeks none save that of the hereafter.

THE GENEROSITY OF THE SAINTS

ST. DOMINIC'S love of books was such that his first biographer tells us they were to him a real necessity of life. Yet he sold these very books so that he might have some money to give to the poor—a sacrifice, says Father Bede Jarrett, that few students in any age would care to make. The saint's own explanation of the sacrifice is this: I could not bear to prize dead skins when living skins were starving and in want.

Fenelon's love of books was no less than St. Dominic's. Yet when his library was burned, he thanked God that it was not the house of a poor man.

When St. Lewis Bertrand was struggling to found his convent in the face of extreme poverty, he poured every penny he could get into the lap of the poor. "Give alms without stint," was his advice to his subjects.

So we read of two of the first followers of St. Dominic that, having begged for a whole day, they managed to collect only a couple of loaves of bread—which they promptly gave to the first beggar they met. "Quite right," said St. Dominic when they made their report to him.

St. Cajetan was another of these reckless people who

threw caution to the winds. He used to say: "We are born and we live not for ourselves but for our neighbors." To those who expostulated with him on account of the prodigality of his almsgiving, he replied: "I shall never cease to give all I can to those in need until I find myself reduced to such a state of poverty, that scarcely will there remain to me five feet of earth for my grave or a penny for my funeral."

St. Ignatius gave away his waistcoat, St. Martin his cloak, St. Francis of Assisi and St. Thomas of Villanova their coats, and the Curé of Ars his shoes. When St. Jean Vianney was alive, Ars was the rendezvous of the miserable and unhappy. "He is the great consoler of the afflicted," it was said at the time. Indeed, he strained the patience of his parishioners with all the hungry people he turned over to them.

St. Vincent de Paul actually went to prison in the place of a condemned criminal. The saints may have made mistakes, may have carried the rigors of penance too far; but at any rate their harshness stopped at their own door. "We must be austere with ourselves and generous with others," said St. John Chrysostom.

St. Ferdinand the king refused to burden his subjects with taxes. "I fear," he said, "the curse of one poor woman more than all the armies of the Moors." Our own St. Alphege was martyred by the Danes because he refused to levy taxes upon his poor people.

St. Gregory the Great abstained from saying Mass for seven days because a poor man died of starvation within the walls of Rome. St. Ambrose settled a pension on the man who tried to assassinate him. St. Romuald pardoned his brother's murderer, and he did that in an age when private vengeance had the sanction of a law.

St. Catherine of Siena became the servant of the woman who slandered her. St. Teresa was also the target of very serious slander, and she excused it by saying that people of strong imaginations often really believe things that have not happened. St. Peter Faber compared himself to the broom of God's house, always employed in sweeping the floor—that is to say, in cleansing the souls of sinners.

THE SACRIFICE OF ST. TELEMACHUS

One of the outstanding heroes of Christian antiquity is St. Telemachus (or Almachus). By a single act of supreme self-sacrifice he put an end once and for all to a social abuse that had lasted for five hundred years—the gladiatorial combats, in which men fought and killed one another in order to provide a diversion for the people.

Caesar is said to have had 320 pairs of gladiators in the arena at one time. The Emperor Trajan forced 10,000 prisoners and gladiators to contend for their lives in the Roman amphitheatre in a spectacle of horror that lasted for 123 days. It was the duty of a Roman magistrate to provide these cruel sports for the people, and many of them made fortunes out of them.

The early Christian Fathers waged a continual struggle against this habit. But the passion was so deep-seated that, as St. Augustine and the fifth-century Christian writer Salvian tell us, even the newly baptized could not restrain themselves from attendance at them. The latter thunders in terrible language against those unworthy converts who find their highest pleasure in seeing men butcher one another in public.

In the East this enormity was suppressed by the Emperor Theodosius. But its abolition in the West was due to the sacrifice of an obscure monk who happened to be a hero.

It is well known how, inspired by one of those tremendous resolutions that sometimes come to saints, Telemachus left his cell in the desert, crossed the sea, arrived in Rome, and gained admittance somehow to the amphitheatre. When the combats were at their height, he leaped the barrier and rushed between the gladiators. Then holding aloft his wooden cross—in the name of Him who shed His blood in order that man might not wantonly shed the blood of his fellow men—he called upon performers and spectators to consider the scandal and the crime of which they were guilty.

The words were hardly out of his mouth when he was cut to pieces by the swords and daggers of the combatants. Some accounts say that he was stoned to death by the spectators. But his sacrifice was not in vain; what sacrifice ever is? His blood was the last to be shed in that arena in which so much had flowed.

This is an extreme of self-sacrificing generosity—Christian charity carried to the highest and most dramatic pitch. People are fond of saying that Christians have not got that sort of stuff in them nowadays. But we are not so sure.

Doubtless there are still plenty of generous souls in our midst living unsuspected by the world at large. In the seventeenth century, Père Charles de Condren, the second General of the Oratory religious order, used to say that he did not believe there were nobler souls in the first centuries than he saw round about him in his own. And yet his own was supposed to be a period of degeneracy.

THE SACRIFICE OF ST. DAMIEN DE VEUSTER

Self-sacrifice can be heroic without being dramatic. At any rate, our modern world of steam and machinery has produced an example of generosity equal to and perhaps even excelling that of Telemachus. Instead of the fifth century, let us take the nineteenth. And in place of a momentary martyrdom, let us take one that lasted for fifteen years.

Telemachus has been the inspiration of literature for fifteen hundred years, providing a festoon of admiration stretching from Theodoret to Fenelon. St. Damien de Veuster, however, excited the pen of one great literary man—Robert Louis Stevenson. This is more or less the gist of Stevenson's *Apologia*.

Damien was only twenty-three when he left his native Belgium in order to dedicate his life to God-alone-knew-what. He was ordained a priest in Honolulu, and then he asked his bishop to allow him to pass over to the Island of Molokai to minister to its lepers. For there were lepers on that Island of Molokai, and there was nobody else. It was simply one large lazaretto.

The lepers had been rounded up in the neighboring islands and segregated on Molokai. There was among them neither priest, doctor, nor nurse. Damien resolved to become all three.

In certain stages, leprosy is an exceedingly infectious disease, and that is the case particularly in the South Seas owing to the ignorance and the habits of the natives. The government of the day was compelled to adopt the peremptory and callous measure of strict sanitary isolation. This island was set apart as a colony, and all those who could be shown to be lepers were forced to take up their abode on it.

Materially their wants were provided for, but morally and socially they were the most unutterably miserable of outcasts. That steaming valley might have become a scene of loathsome riotousness. To the physical distemper there might have been added the foulness of immorality and of vice. Eight hundred men and women with no superior, no guide, no religion, no hope—eight hundred hearts with nothing in them except indignation, resentment, and despair.

It was Damien who averted that peril and that curse. He taught them how to suffer. By accepting to live among them, he demonstrated that their lot was not intolerable.

He wished to make them believe that their disease was not a brand of infamy but a badge of honor—that Jesus Christ Himself was willing to be compared to a leper, and that on His cross He hardly looked like anything else. And that lesson Damien only succeeded in teaching them when he had contracted the disease himself.

This need not surprise us. Our Lord was able to make suffering and death valuable and intelligible to us by suffering and dying Himself.

"ALL THINGS TO ALL MEN"

Damien was given permission, this young man of twenty-three, and on May 25, 1873, he set out. He was pulled ashore by the marines one early morning, and as the boat drew near the landing stage, he saw the pier and the stairs crowded with those terrible deformations of our common humanity. He saw what Our Lord saw long ago when He looked down into the Valley of Hinnom; what He saw when it was said to Him: "Lord, if You will, You can make me clean" (Mt 8:1–2).

He saw himself landing and living in the midst of such a population as only now and then surrounds us in the chill horror of a bad dream. Then and then only the significance of what he was undertaking began to dawn upon his mind. He was only a young man.

"Why should I do this? What ails me that I should want to do this thing?" Is it any wonder that in imagination he cast a haggard glance back at the pleasant fields and the Old World cities of his native Belgium?

Then he jumped ashore and bade farewell forever to the decencies and the refinements of civilization. With his own hand, he slammed the door of his own sepulcher.

That first night he slept under a tree in the midst of his rotting brethren—alone on that island with pestilence for his companion and looking forward, with God-alone-knows what sinking of the heart, to fifteen years of dressing sores and stumps. The story of those fifteen years is an old story and a familiar one.

For fifteen years that man lived in the waste of the waters with leprosy and lepers for his associates. It was in the year 1885 that he discovered the unmistakable signs of the disease on his own person. And yet he was able to thank God.

"Now," he said, "when I preach I shall be able to say instead of 'dear brethren,' 'my fellow lepers.'" And in his last letter to his acquaintance Edward Clifford, he writes: "I try my best to carry without much complaining . . . the long-foreseen miseries of the disease, which, after all, is a providential agent to detach the heart from all earthly affection."

Just before he died, with two priests and the Sisters of Charity to continue his work, he concluded: "The work of the lepers is assured, and I am no longer necessary."

When his assistant priest asked him if he would, like Elias, leave his mantle behind him to inspire his successors, he replied: "Why? What would you do with it? It is full of leprosy." [88]

The malady had concentrated itself in his mouth and throat. As he lay in his hut on the seashore, and as the noise of the waves grew fainter and fainter in his diseased ears, he had to look to heaven for his consolation, for this earth had misunderstood him, and it had done even worse: It had impugned his motives and assailed his character.

"All things to all men" (1 Cor 9:22). Did St. Paul know what strength of mind and generosity of character he might be demanding when he laid down that sublime rule of perfection?

What are we to think of a missionary who goes out

88 Clifford, 111–114.

not only to live among leprosy, but to become a leper—who accepts to be numbered among eight hundred men and women in various stages of a disease that has been the nightmare of history and is still the conundrum of medical science?[89] What, indeed, are we to think except that the flame of generous self-sacrifice still burns in Catholic hearts!

89 Effective treatment for leprosy (Hansen's Disease) first appeared in the late 1940s, after this book was published.

THE SUFFERINGS OF THE SAINTS

LITERATURE has exhausted itself in extolling suffering and depicting the benefits it brings to those who accept it. François Coppée wrote his *La Belle Souffrance* and Oscar Wilde wrote his *De Profundis* in order to tell the world what pain and misfortune had done for them. The poet William Wordsworth speaks of "the soothing thoughts that spring out of human suffering,"[90] and the poet John Keats says of sorrow:

> I thought to leave thee
> And deceive thee
> And now of all the world I love thee best.[91]

Henrietta Maria of England used to thank God for having made her an unhappy queen because suffering had taught her a lesson that royalty could never have taught her.

One shrewd critic of Napoleon Bonaparte considers that he was altogether unfortunate in that he had never

90 From William Wordsworth, "Intimations of Immortality From Recollections of Early Childhood."

91 From John Keats, "Song of the Indian Maid."

really learned to struggle against adversity. He had only been half-educated in the effects that events produce upon great men. Prosperity had accompanied him far too long. He had escaped the deceptions and chastisements, and therefore the lessons, of destiny.

"We get a charm from sorrow," says Bishop Jacques-Bénigne Bossuet; and again: "Sorrow is the vesture of those who love."

An English essayist has noted: Although prosperity is the great blessing of the Old Testament, as adversity is the great blessing of the New Testament, yet even in the Old Testament the sacred writers have labored more in describing the afflictions of Job than in depicting the felicity of Solomon.

PREACHING SUFFERING BY EXAMPLE

But the saints did more than extol suffering in prose and verse. They preached the difficult and unacceptable truth concerning it by their example. They demonstrated by their lives the providential mission of pain to the soul of man.

They anticipated the chance discoveries that people like Wilde and Coppée made at the end of an irregular and thoughtless life. They went resolutely to meet suffering, deliberately chose it for a companion, and travelled in its company all the time.

St. Teresa called each trial that came to her "a little present from God." When her broken arm was being set in a very painful manner, she sent all the sisters out of the room. When they came in afterwards, they found her radiant. "I would not have missed it," she said, "for the whole world." So true it is that a saint's sufferings never get in other people's way.

The French apologist Father Louis Gaston de Segur asked God to send him the biggest trial He could send. God sent him blindness. He had asked for this as a favor, and as a favor he accepted it.

"Will you come with Me to Golgotha?" Our Lord asked St. Lydwine.

"Indeed I shall," was the answer. "I am ready to accompany You to the mountain and to suffer and die there with You."

When St. Lydwine was asked whether she desired to get better, she answered: "No, there is but one thing now that I desire: It is not to be deprived of my discomforts and pains."

When her maladies devoured her, St. Veronica Guiliani would cry out: "Long live the sacred Cross; long live suffering!"

St. Teresa of the Infant Jesus did not know how she would get used to a heaven in which there is no suffering.

"Always to suffer and to die," said St. Teresa; and St. Mary Magdalen of Pazzi corrected this into "always to suffer and not to die." "Still more, O Lord, still more," exclaimed St. Francis Xavier as he lay suffering on the shores of China. Mère Marie de Bourg, founder of the Congregation of the Savior and the Blessed Virgin Mary, used to say to her spiritual daughters: "If they sold pain in the market, I would go quickly and fetch some."

"Most of our sufferings," said Blessed Henry Suso, "we make for ourselves." And he tells an amusing story of a pious man who was making too much of his aches and pains. Passing a house, he heard the anguished cries of a woman.

"Ah," he thought, "here is a poor soul in torment. I shall go and console her."

"Ah, my poor woman," he said when he got inside, "what ails you?"

"I have let my needle drop and I can't find it."

However, the saints were well above this childish pettiness. St. Teresa sternly forbade her sisters to ask God for help in the trivial trials of every day. "There is no necessity to go praying for patience to bear a headache," she would say.

When St. Julie Billiart made her foundation at Ghent, she had seven nuns on her hands and only four beds to go round. Yet they enjoyed themselves sleeping on the floor with bundles of sticks for pillows. They had only bread for supper, and when it got moldy, she would bless it and tell them to get on with it. "It never did us any harm," one of the sisters said.

We must not judge the sufferings of the saints by our own capacity to bear pain, but by theirs. The great victims among them were expert and highly trained in the matter of endurance. They were planted in a far richer soil than are we, and they drew from that soil a strength of which we have no experience.

We are unmanned by our own timidity and by the softness of modern life. No people suffer more acutely than the shrinking sort. On the other hand, the terrors of hardship simply melt away before a resolute and brave character.

The strangest name in the calendar of the saints is

that of St. Quodvultdeus, which means in Latin "Whatever God wills." He was an African bishop who was banished from Carthage by the Arian Vandal king Genseric. He received his nickname on account of the extraordinary facility with which he adapted himself to adversity.

MISFORTUNE, A SEASON OF GRACE

Providentially, seasons of trial and crises of misfortune have been seasons of grace and spiritual enlightenment. This is what the Italian poet Dante meant when he said that sorrow remarries us to God. And this is what the poet Francis Thompson meant when he wrote:

> Ah! Must—
> Designer infinite!—
> Ah! must Thou char the wood
> Ere Thou canst limn with it?[92]

Grace without suffering to enhance it is simply income and not capital. And no one's face can be set in the direction of heaven if it is not first set in the direction of Calvary.

Moses was languishing in exile when God spoke to him from the burning bush. Daniel was in captivity in Babylon when the gift of prophecy came to him. Manasseh was brought to God by disaster. St. John was a prisoner in Patmos when he was caught up to heaven to see "what no eye has seen, nor ear heard" (1 Cor 2:9).

---

92 From "The Hound of Heaven" in *The Complete Poetical Works of Francis Thompson* (New York: Boni & Liveright, 1923), 92.

Who never ate his bread in sorrow,
Who never spent the midnight hours,
Weeping and waiting for the morrow;
He knows ye not, ye heavenly powers.[93]

It was while he was suffering in a dungeon at Toledo that St. John of the Cross received the most valuable of his spiritual illuminations. Like Boethius he could have said: "God and my prison have made me what I am." And had it not been for this persecution we might never have had his incomparable *Living Flame,* which carries mystical experience perhaps as high as it has ever been carried.

SUFFERING AND CONVERSION

We see from the lives of the saints that time and again it was in the moment of defeat and failure that many of them began to lead a life worth living, or to apply themselves seriously to tasks of spiritual perfection. Disaster in many cases released their tears, tears which they had refused to shed for so long and which were destined to purify and to heal them.

Trials and misfortune were the springboard by which Blessed Angela of Foligno rose to sanctity. A married woman, she lived in adultery and shame. Then began an appalling process of purification.

In blow after blow she lost her mother, her husband, her children. During two years the Devil sifted her like wheat. Then she divided her goods among the poor and assumed the habit of the Third Order of St. Francis.

93 See Johann Wolfgang von Goethe, *Wilhelm Meister's Apprenticeship*, II, 13.

St. Rita of Cascia similarly was widowed and bereft of her children at an early age. But just when her life seemed to have lost its purpose and meaning, grace came to her rescue and enabled her to begin all over again in an even better way. It was the same sort of domestic tragedy that enriched the Early Church with three of the most illustrious women that are to be found in the calendar of the saints.

St. Melania and her husband were persons of great wealth and prominent in the Roman society of their time. Having lost by death their two children, they resolved on embracing a life of evangelical perfection. Selling all their possessions and distributing the proceeds among the poor, they established themselves in Palestine in monasteries that they themselves had founded.

St. Paula in the same way dedicated her widowhood to the service of God to such purpose that St. Jerome was able to describe her as "the precious jewel of the Church."

St. Marcella was bereaved after seven months of married life, upon which she concentrated all her thoughts upon the things of eternity.

Of these three courageous women, St. Jerome says that adversity enabled them to achieve a twofold and unusual triumph—a victory over the natural weakness of their sex and a victory over the ties of affection.

St. Hyacintha of Mariscotti, the patron of Viterbo, as a young girl was bent upon marriage and a worldly life. But being disappointed in love, she retired to a convent at the age of twenty. Here for ten years she led a life of tepidity until an illness that nearly proved fatal induced her to give herself up wholly to God. Suffering had converted her twice, and for the remainder of her life, suffering was her vocation.

St. Peter Gonzalez, who is the patron saint of Spanish seafaring men, began life as a worldly and ambitious ecclesiastic interested merely in the professional side of religion. Being appointed dean of the chapter of Astorga, he came dressed up in expensive clothes and mounted on a splendid horse to take possession of his appointment. The horse, however, stumbled in the presence of the spectators and threw the young dean into a drain.

This humiliation brought him to his senses. He retired from the world in order to learn the will of God in solitude. Afterwards he entered the Order of St. Dominic.

St. Alphonsus Liguori was a barrister before he became a priest. The last case that he defended in the law courts of Naples was an important one, so important indeed that the plaintiffs would entrust it to no other hands but his. However, by an extraordinary oversight, he totally mismanaged and lost it.

"World! Henceforward I know you not," were his words as soon as he recovered from the first shock of his disappointment. He did indeed break with the world, and few ever broke with it so completely.

The conversion of St. Ignatius Loyola was worked out in accordance with the very same providential plan. It was an accident—an accident resulting in disablement and disfigurement that gave him and his Society to the Church.

St. Alonzo Rodriguez lost his wife and little son after four years of happy married life. All for him was finished in a sense; but only in one sense. In a better sense all was about to begin. With the setting of the worldly life, the eternal life dawned for him as for Dante. With the collapse of his temporal affairs he accepted the Gospel paradox that teaches man to gain his life by losing it.

SUFFERING AND CHARITY

The very goodness and charity of the saints involved them in suffering, no doubt on the principle that good is never done in this world save at the personal expense of those who try to do it.

St. Joseph Cupertino was slandered by those whom he had befriended.

St. John Facundus was poisoned by a woman whose paramour he had ventured to rebuke.

Our own Blessed Edmund Arrowsmith owed his martyrdom to his zeal for setting right an irregular marriage.

Blessed Henry Suso was scandalously defamed by a woman whom he had protected and tried to reform.

It has been said of St. John of the Cross that it was his vocation to suffer at the hands of his own brethren. Certainly, he had more than his share of this most difficult of all trials.

We are so apt to make up our minds that religious and spiritual people have simply no right to ill treat or to misjudge us. But we forget that it is only in heaven that there will be no misunderstandings.

St. William of York was kept from taking possession of his see by his own archdeacon. For ten years he lived in retirement at Winchester while the archdeacon enjoyed his victory. Being reelected at length and receiving the pallium, he once more attempted to take possession of his archbishopric.

The archdeacon, however, met him on the way and forbade him to enter the town. In fact he lived for only a few weeks more. At the time, his death was attributed to poisoning.

St. Thomas of Hereford was excommunicated on his deathbed by his own primate.

St. Alphonsus was excluded from the religious order he had founded, and on one occasion his own fathers reported to the king a joke about the Neapolitan Court that he had made at recreation.

St. Mary Magdalene was thrice misunderstood—by the Pharisees, by Martha,[94] and by Judas, and thrice was she vindicated and each time by Our Lord Himself.

Fortunately for the saints, their vindication was always in the same safe and divine hands.

VICTIM SOULS

There is a multitude of saintly sufferers who are in a class by themselves. All through the Christian ages there have been found rare and special souls willing to pay the ransom for the sins and vices of men. As St. Catherine of Siena said in dying: "O Eternal God, accept the sacrifice of my life for the mystical body of Your holy Church."

This providential arrangement has been called the law of equilibrium between good and evil, the balance

94 Though the identification of Mary Magdalene (Lk 8:2) with Mary, the sister of Martha in the Gospel (Lk 10:39), has been common in the West, since ancient times in the East they have usually been seen as two different persons.

between virtue and vice. As reparation for the sins of the many, God claims the penances of the few. When the needle of the compass inclines too much to the wrong side, when wrongdoing becomes too obtrusive, God's mercy is such that He excites the generosity of His elect living on earth and makes of them willing victims of expiation. Were it not for this counterpoise of voluntary penance the universe might long ago have been in ruins.

St. Frances of Rome, for example, was raised up as a sacrificial victim to atone for the sins of her age.

Blessed Osanne, the patroness of the town of Mantua in Italy, was only seven years old when Our Lord appeared to her and placed His cross upon her shoulders and predicted for her a life of torture.

St. Catherine of Genoa was torn from head to foot by supernatural infirmities. She experienced the torments of the Passion and endured the fires of purgatory to save souls.

St. Mary Magdalen of Pazzi besought Our Lord to burden her with the sins of the world, and she was taken at her word.

Marguerite of the Blessed Sacrament, the French Carmelite, was raised up to expiate by her maladies the offences done to God by lack of charity among the rich.

To another French Carmelite, Marie Angelique de la Providence, Our Lord actually showed the sinners whose offences He wished her to neutralize by her sufferings.

Anna Maria Taigi sacrificed herself more especially for the persecutors of the Church.

Supreme among all these, however, stands the figure of the incomparable St. Lydwine of Schiedam. She fell on the ice while skating and broke one of her ribs. From this time to her death, forty years later, she was bedridden.

During the greater part of the period she lived in a cellar, taking no solid food, and praying and weeping so that in winter her tears formed two frozen streams upon her cheeks. She was afflicted with almost every known physical disorder. "She was a fruit of expiation which God pressed until He had extracted from it the very last drop."

Her insatiable desire to make reparation loaded her with ills. She reenacted the anguish of Calvary. She was nailed to the empty cross and became the counterpart of the Crucified.

When she first fell ill her confessor said to her: "Say to Jesus: 'I wish to place myself of my own will upon Your cross, and I wish it should be You who drive in the nails.' He will accept this office of executioner, and the angels will assist Him."

Lydwine's eyes were opened, and she gratefully and humbly accepted the mission that Our Lord had imposed upon her. For thirty-eight years she never swerved from that mysterious path of mystic substitution, until at last Our Lord came to her, restored her body to its former soundness, gave her back the beauty of her youth, and Himself administered to her the sacrament of Extreme Unction.[95] Then He remained visibly beside her until she died.

The English martyr St. John Houghton was hung and then cut down while still alive to endure the most

95 The Sacrament of Extreme Unction is now called Anointing of the Sick.

barbarous part of the execution: disembowelment. As the executioner tore open his chest to remove his heart, the saint was heard to say: "Good Jesus, what will You do with my heart?"

And what indeed could Our Lord do with that poor heart except place it next and near His own? This and nothing less than this was the assurance that supported the saints in the midst of their sufferings.

THE ENLIGHTENMENT OF THE SAINTS

WE CANNOT deny that in many ways the saints were the children of their own time and even place. St. John of the Cross was a Spaniard, and the Spanish genius is plainly reflected in his mysticism. Blessed John Ruysbroeck belonged to the North, and there is in his mysticism a notable and valuable element that St. John of the Cross lacked and that is in accord with the temperament of the northerner.

So, again, all the Italian mystics of the thirteenth century reflect the spirit of Italy and of St. Francis. It has been said of the *Mystical City* of Marie d'Agreda that it smells of periwigs and ruffles and the Court of Louis XIV. St. Alphonsus was a real Neapolitan, and St. Philip Neri was a Florentine of the Florentines.

"I am a Lombard," St. Paul of the Cross was fond of saying. "I am a Lombard and I detest dissimulation. What I have in my heart I have also on my tongue."

As for St. Teresa, she has been well described as embodying "all that is noblest, most representative, in the Castilian character—a character famed for its stern self-repression, its endurance, rectitude, sobriety, dignified simplicity and austerity, its grave and stately courtesy."[96]

This, of course, need not surprise us. It is not at all necessary that we cease to be ourselves in order to become pleasing to God. Grace is never the obliteration of nature, and the highest sanctity leaves the personality and the individuality intact.

St. Paul was never at any pains to conceal what he was, and he had a real pride in the city which gave him birth. "I am a Jew, from Tarsus in Cilicia, a citizen of no mean city" (Acts 21:39). He was even energetic in the assertion of his political rights: "Is it lawful for you to scourge a man who is a Roman citizen, and uncondemned?" (Acts 22:25).

SUBJECTED TO THEIR AGE AND ENVIRONMENT

To some extent the saints were *subjected* to their age and environment. They shared its limitations and were forced by their circumstances to be patient with the shortcomings of their period and surroundings.

St. Alphonsus' bad tooth was extracted by the local barber armed with a razor, and he had no anesthetic except his crucifix. St. Teresa's broken arm was mended in the usual sixteenth-century fashion. And St. Francis of Assisi had to put up with the horrors of the medieval method of cauterization, praying all the while that the fire might not be too unkind.

---

96 Gabriela Cunninghame Graham, *Santa Teresa: Being Some Account of Her Life and Times* (London: Adam and Charles Black, 1894), II, 2.

The English bishop who visited St. Lydwine of Schiedam and questioned her as to her state, received this very sensible answer: "Alas! Monseigneur, I am obliged to live among secular people and cannot avoid being mixed up in the affairs of the world. I am polluted by the dust that springs up round the people of the age."

St. Peter Claver devoted himself with amazing personal charity to alleviating the lot of the slaves. But there is no evidence that he ever denounced the slave trade itself. Had he done so, he would probably have been banished and an end made of all his charitable ministrations.

Neither his time nor place was ripe for a profitable discussion of the essential injustice of slavery. So St. Peter Claver, not being able to do all he wanted to do, was content to do what he could. He *accepted* the position without in the least acquiescing in it.

St. Vincent de Paul sat patiently in the antechamber of the Court of Versailles, which he knew to be a scandalous court. He did not denounce its open licentiousness. To do so would have been to ruin the cause of the poor. It was his business to relieve the poverty that was rife in the Paris of his day, and he decided to mind his own business.

SUPERIOR TO THEIR TIME AND PLACE

But at the same time and to a notable extent the saints were *superior* to their time and place. Some of them advanced very far indeed beyond the frontiers of their own horizon. It has been remarked of St. Teresa of Ávila that, although she was Spanish, she was so complex and many-sided that race seems almost obliterated in her.

The German theologian Karl Adam says of St.

Augustine that because of his psychological habit of mind, he is "so near to the modern man, nearer than any of the great scholastics. . . . He is still more modern in his life, that is to say in the special manner in which he lived his life, in its special rhythm and quality."[97]

St. Jerome again has been called the most original personality of the fourth century and the most modern character of ancient times. There is certainly a very up-to-date flavor about these words from his letter to Furia: "What business has a Christian to cover her face with paint? . . . How can she weep for her sins when her tears have to force their way through it? . . . What right has she to raise to heaven a face which her Creator cannot recognize?"[98]

Again, the portrait of St. Monica that has come down to us from the fourth century is essentially a medieval portrait. Florence or Venice in the age of Dante or Petrarch seems a more natural background for this woman at once so tender and so strong, rather than Africa in the age of the Vandals.

In his *European Civilization*, Jaime Balmes says of St. Bernard: "Here is a man formed entirely and exclusively under the influence of Catholicity . . . who never dreamed of setting his intellect free from the yoke of authority; and yet he rises like a mighty pyramid above all the men of his time."[99]

---

97 Karl Adam, *St. Augustine: The Odyssey of His Soul*, Justin McCann, trans. (London: Sheed and Ward, 1932), 7–8.

98 Jerome, Letter LIV, "To Furia," 7.

99 J[aime] Balmes, *European Civilization: Protestantism and Catholicity Compared* (Baltimore: Murphy, 1859), 422.

Even the historian Edward Gibbon was struck by those characteristics in Bernard that we usually describe as "advanced" or "superior." "In speech, in writing, in action," he says, "Bernard stood high above his rivals and contemporaries. . . . The abbot of Clairvaux became the oracle of Europe."[100]

So too in her *Legends of the Monastic Orders,* Anna Jameson describes St. Teresa as "the most extraordinary woman of her age and country."[101] "A genius of superb originality" is another tribute that comes from a non-Catholic source.

PEOPLE OF VISION

Indeed, many of the saints must be given credit for a real enlightenment of mind that carried them far ahead of their generation. They had what is called "vision," an insight or perception quite special and to which their contemporaries were strangers. They were deaf to the little motives of little men and blind to the petty views of petty men.

Non est inventus similis illi, the Church says of them, in order to indicate their originality: "Nothing like them can be found."

They were distinguished people, exceptional people. And for that very reason they were commonly out of joint with their age, disliked and distrusted by all "sensible" persons, regarded as oddities—as men and women

100 Gibbon, X, 285.

101 [Anna] Jameson, *Legends of the Monastic Orders, as represented in the Fine Arts* (London: Longman, Brown, Green, and Longmans, 1852), 415.

with "ideas" and "notions." "Why can't you act like everybody else?" is the reproach we find brought against them by their contemporaries.

St. Catherine of Siena was accused of making a virtue of her own uniqueness. St. Francis of Assisi was looked upon with extreme disfavor by all sorts of prominent personages. And the Curé of Ars was unanimously voted a "freak" by the majority of his fellow priests.

The truth is that sanctity is a real illumination of the mind. Sanctity can do what scholastic learning may never do. St. Thomas Aquinas always maintained that he learnt more at the feet of his crucifix than he did in his books. The Irish writer Oliver Goldsmith described himself at one period of his life as having a stock of learning that would have puzzled a philosopher and a degree of ignorance of which a schoolboy would have been ashamed.

What after all can *they* know of life who are ignorant of the meaning and purpose of life? Unless the end is determined, nothing is determined; and blindness to the objective is a serious handicap to the understanding of life itself. It was a very learned modern scholar who described human existence as a game of blind man's buff.

So much for the insufficiency of modern scholarship. But the saints never felt that they were just groping about in the dark. There was no "dark" and no "groping." They walked forward resolutely like the "children of the light" that they were, anticipating discoveries that had not been made and arriving at conclusions while those around them were still squabbling about principles and premises.

It is only necessary to read the *Utopia* of St. Thomas More to realize that he was indeed "one born out of due time" (1 Cor 15:8 Douay-Rheims). The social and religious evils that More attacks in this book were so generally acquiesced in and so far from being recognized as evils that, in the interests of self-protection, he had to cast his work in a fantastic and paradoxical mold. He had some very unpleasant and unacceptable truths to put before the authorities of both Church and state, and therefore he found it necessary to mix up the serious and the absurd, the sublime and the ridiculous.

St. Thomas More was head and shoulders above his times. He was a real rebel in revolt against injustice that he condemned in the name of Christianity, and that posterity, enlightened by painful experience, has been compelled to condemn in the name of social expediency.

It is sometimes said that we owe nearly all the conveniences of modern life to the enlightenment of our forefathers. It would be truer to say that we owe them to the enlightenment of *some* of our forefathers. Just as the history of the world is in reality the history of a few powerful men, so the story of progress is in reality the story of a few pioneers; and many of the saints deserve a foremost place in the list of those pioneers.

They did manage to shake themselves free of that almost imperceptible tyranny that custom and usage impose upon us. There is certainly no servitude like the servitude that subjects you to views you know to be false, and to habits of living you know to be absurd. And it redounds to the credit of these saints that they did succeed in escaping clean out of the network of opinion in which their contemporaries were enmeshed.

They disdained the commonplace grooves of

convention and were not at all disposed to do things just because they saw them being done. Illumined as they were by the divine wisdom, they became the luminaries of their age. Thus the *Chronicles of Windersheim* says of the Flemish Mystic Gerard Groote: "The world at this time was growing old, and set upon the way that leads downwards to hell, when Providence made ready a light and a lamp."[102]

SAINTS AND THE ANIMALS

The saints did serve as lamps to their generation, although their generation was often heedless of the fact. Posterity, however, on looking back recognizes how much the cause of reformation and improvement owes to these men and women.

What a debt we owe to saints such as Francis of Assisi! Here is a man of the thirteenth century who is able to give the twentieth century some pointers. The twentieth-century "average good Christian" does not know where he is on the elementary question of his relationship to the animal creation. But St. Francis of Assisi knew where *he* was on the same elementary question.

This "average good Christian" of the twentieth century has been told so often that the animals have "no rights." He has been warned so often that he must be very, very, very careful not to get sentimental about them. So he has come to believe that this emphatic "No Rights!" and this emphatic "No Sentiment!" have settled

102 The fifteenth-century *Chronicles of Windesheim* were written by Johannes Buschius, a contemporary of Thomas à Kempis.

the matter between them.

"*Causa finita est*—the case is closed! So let's get on with our hunting and our trapping and our vivisecting and our maiming and laming and big game shooting. Animals can have no rights, so evidently they can suffer no wrongs. How very sensible our religion is!"

Draw the attention of this average good Christian to cruelties that fashion demands, that custom sanctions, that the law allows, that society insists upon calling "good sport," and that science exploits to the utmost in the interests of its own exceedingly dubious ends. At once he wraps himself up and makes himself snug and comfortable in the little jacket of his "No Sentiment."

The Italians, apparently, go one better. "They are not Christians," they say when you reprimand them for their cruelty to bird or beast. This is a curious reversal of the teaching of the Qur'an of Muhammad that more or less insinuates that Christians have "no rights." The "chivalrous Spanish nation," with even more subtle ingenuity, maintains that the bulls "simply love it."

But these animals of ours certainly make up for their lack of rights by the abundance of the wrongs against them, and many of the saints were far ahead of us in their realization and abhorrence of these wrongs. This is what St. Bonaventure tells us about St. Francis:

> He considered all created beings as coming from the paternal heart of God. This community of origin made him feel a real fraternity with them all. He said: "They have the same source as we have. Like us, they derive the life of thought, will, and love

> from the Creator. Not to hurt our humble brethren is our first duty to them; but to stop there is a complete misapprehension of the intentions of Providence. We have a higher mission. God wishes that we should succor them whenever they require it."[103]

St. Bonaventure himself makes no attempt to conceal or to apologize for the friendship which St. Francis had for the birds and beasts. He sympathizes with it and he ennobles it by his own lofty appreciation. This in itself is a testimony to his *own* enlightenment and his superiority to that dread of being thought sentimental which, no doubt, was the bugbear of his day as it is of ours.

In the eyes of Francis, he says, "all created beings were like so many streams flowing from that source of boundless love from which he would fain drink, and their diverse virtues seemed to him to form a celestial harmony to which his soul was attuned."[104]

Centuries before, they had not hesitated to incorporate this beautiful prayer in the Liturgy of St. Basil.

> O God, enlarge within us the sense of fellowship with all living things, our little brothers to whom Thou hast given this earth as their home in common with us. We remember with shame that in the

---

103 This quote has been widely circulated, but usually without citation of a source. On the rare occasion when a source is given, it is St. Bonaventure's *Life of St. Francis of Assisi* (see n. 104 below). But the quote is nowhere to be found in that text, so it may well be apocryphal or misattributed.

104 Compare the translation by Henry Edward in St. Bonaventure, *The Life of S. Francis of Assisi: From the "Legenda Santi Francisci" of S. Bonaventure* (London: R. Washbourne, 1868), 111.

past we have exercised the high dominion of man with ruthless cruelty, so that the voice of the earth which should have gone up to Thee in song has been a groan of travail. May we realize that they live, not for us alone, but for themselves and for Thee, and that they love the sweetness of life even as we, and serve Thee better in their place than we in ours.[105]

"A HELLISH PLEASURE"

With us, apparently, the question of blood sports is still an open question, and one which no doubt we find it far too inconvenient to settle with a Christian answer. But St. Francis de Sales in the sixteenth century was quite emphatic on the point. A "hellish pleasure" is the name he gave to the hunting chase that has no motive save amusement.

Our trouble, of course, is that our judgment is warped by custom. Our minds are Christian enough and Catholic, but beneath the surface of this mind of ours there is what is called an "under-mind"; and unfortunately this "under-mind" may be, without our knowing it, quite

---

105 Although various portions of this prayer have been widely attributed to the Eastern liturgy of St. Basil, it does not seem to appear anywhere there, in any of that liturgy's various forms. However, these exact words (in English) appear in a collection of prayers by the American Baptist theologian Walter Rauschenbusch, a leading figure in the so-called "Social Gospel" movement at the turn of the twentieth century. See *Prayers of the Social Awakening* (New York: Pilgrim Press, 1910), 47–48. In it, Rauschenbusch seems to suggest that the prayers collected there are his own, and he does not attribute these particular words to the liturgy of St. Basil or any other source.

un-Christian and un-Catholic. This explains why those who are apparently sound believers can go on associating themselves with ways of thinking and acting that are utterly foreign to the real Christian spirit.

The Fathers of the Desert were ministered to by lions and tigers. St. Gall ruled over the bears in the Alps like a superior over a body of docile monks. The very vultures played with St. Columbanus.

The wolf of Gubbio never molested St. Francis; the lion of Bethlehem never molested St. Jerome. The mosquitoes that helped St. Rose of Lima to sing the Divine Office never stung their little patroness and protector. St. Jerome tells us that although St. Pachomius the Hermit lived in a cave infested by poisonous reptiles, yet he never suffered any harm, and the fiercest of crocodiles offered themselves to him and often carried him on their backs across the Nile.

These stories used to cause a great deal of amusement. But of late quite intelligent people are beginning to apply themselves to the study of these curious incidents in the lives of the ascetics and to suspect that they contain a fruitful lesson that the world in general may yet learn. The whole traditional and accepted attitude of man to the animal kingdom is now being closely interrogated.

It begins to be felt that these saints possessed a wisdom, a sound psychological insight, to which we moderns have not as yet even remotely approached: In short, the ferocity of man is largely responsible for the ferocity of the brutes, and in the presence of God's servants the fiercest of beasts do not feel the instinctive dread with which our depravity and lack of sympathy inspires them.

"I will wear nothing that has cost suffering," said a modern saint. It has taken us fairly long to reach this stage of enlightenment, and millions have not reached it even yet. The fashionable modern woman continues to make herself directly responsible for atrocities that cover our civilization with shame.

The plumage is still torn from the living bird at a time when it is rearing its young, in order to adorn the head-dress of society ladies. Sheep are beaten with iron rods to induce premature labor, so that the idle woman may wear the soft coat of the lamb that is born. Cruelty never exists except where there is lack of courage, and the saints had that sort of courage that society would most likely appraise as heroic—the courage to defy fashion.

SAINTLY WOMEN OF VISION

The Norwegian playwright Henrik Ibsen wrote his *Doll's House* to emphasize the fact that the average woman of his day was living in an unreal world—a slave to the petty futilities of domesticity, to the ignoble routine of dressing and undressing, of simpering and tea-pouring and chattering from morning to night about less than nothing at all. But far better than Ibsen's play, the lives of St. Catherine of Siena, of St. Teresa of Ávila, of St. Bridget of Sweden, demonstrate that another conception of life is possible to a woman if only she will be strong-minded enough to take hold of it.

"O admirable woman," wrote Thomas of Celano of St. Clare—admirable not on account of her ecstasies and miracles, but by reason of that elevation of character that lifted her right above the usual petty level of her sex.

St. Julie Billiart was another of those women who had the strength of mind "to cut the thongs of their own futility." Nothing could be more robust, more virile than her familiar exhortations and letters: "Never will I suffer among us those souls without courage, those womanish hearts that can endure nothing. There must be nothing little among us. A religious must not be taken up with a headache, with those thousand and one aches and pains to which we are subject."[106]

St. Juliana of Falconieri even as a young girl had fortitude enough to break the slavery of custom—of doing "the usual things" and "what is expected of one." Of exceptional beauty and attractiveness, she battled hard in order to adhere to her resolution of remaining single against the opposition of a narrow-minded mother who resorted to violent abuse and blows. St. Rose of Lima had the same sort of mother to contend with, and she gained a victory unusual in a girl of her age—a victory over dress and cosmetics.

Gabriel Cozzano, who was St. Angela Merici's secretary, says of her that "her burning spirit pierced the spheres and stood unabashed before God." Yet this woman of prayer and contemplation was far ahead of her time in the practical matter of school management. She actually had "views" about girls' education.

She anticipated recent theories in counseling the avoidance of force and in asserting that the school ought to be the transplanted and transformed home. Her entire

---

106 The probable source of this quote is *The Life of Blessed Julie Billiart, Founder of the Institute of Sisters of Notre Dame, by a Member of the Same Society*, Fr. James Clare, S.J., ed. (London: Sands, 1909).

system was based upon the great principle enunciated by the German educator Friedrich Froebel: The child learns not by studying justice and responsibility in casual relations, but by trying them out!

DEBATABLE QUESTIONS

For that matter, St. John Bosco was also quite advanced in his notions of education. In 1877 he wrote: "During forty years I do not remember having used formal punishment!"

St. Bernard rescued a criminal from the hangman. "Give him to me," he said. "I will put him to death with my own hands." His idea, of course, was to reform him, to kill the old man in him and make him a new creature.

"Do you want to save the Devil himself?" the magistrate asked. "You little know what a reckless ruffian you are about to let loose upon society."

Bernard, however, had his way, and the hangman lost his job for that once at least. He took the prisoner to Clairvaux and made a first-rate monk of him. Is it seriously suggested that St. Bernard was opposed on principle to capital punishment? He may have been. Why not?[107]

These matters which we insist on calling "debatable questions" may not be so very debatable at all. Perhaps we find it possible to argue about them simply because we do not give our Christian conscience a chance. We regard the tortures and burnings of the past with amazement,

---

107 The author's question about capital punishment, posed in 1936, is especially noteworthy in light of recent developments in the Church's teaching; see the *Catechism of the Catholic Church*, 2267.

but Christian posterity a century hence may regard our social and humanitarian views with an amazement even greater still.

THE DIET OF THE SAINTS

AN INTERESTING aspect of the enlightenment of the saints is their sane and, as we should say nowadays, their advanced theories regarding diet. In this respect they seem to have been much wiser than are we. They did have a reasoned view about food, while most of us have none. They went their own independent way, while we allow ourselves to be stampeded by custom, by the advertiser, by the whole mass suggestion of the age we live in.

Certainly the trend of modern enlightened nutritional science is an endorsement of the wisdom of the saints. They have been accused of being dirty, and certainly travel-stained and grimy many of them were. But at any rate they did not defile themselves as do we with the abominations of commercialized food.

It has been said that if the great mystics and ascetics lived in our century they would eat whatever is popular fare. One wonders. There is no evidence that these great saints were ever inclined to eat what was popular fare. Blessed Charles de Foucauld, it is true, was persuaded to accept some cans of condensed milk. But he merely tasted it in order to please his friends while adhering rigidly to his diet of dates and vegetables.

It is certainly a grievous error to suppose that the saints simply did not care what they threw down their throats. Their entire history is a refutation of that notion. On the contrary, they were faddists about food in the best sense of the word. They were faddists about food because they were not pagans but good Christians.

St. Dominic's diet was very carefully regulated. He was very fond of apples and turnips. When he could arrange his own diet he invariably ate vegetables, bread, and soup. When he dined at the houses of those who gave him hospitality, he allowed his hosts to please themselves, but he confined himself to a couple of eggs or a small piece of dried fish with wine two-thirds watered.

St. Gilbert of Sempringham drew up careful rules of diet for his nuns. The weaker ones were to have a light breakfast of ale and bread. But the normal regulation was one chief meal at midday consisting of eggs, fruit, and honey.

Certainly one and all the saints were enemies of what they called "singularity"—that is, peculiarity that draws attention to itself. But this word "singularity" requires very careful defining. The imperfect and lackadaisical are often fond of excusing themselves on the plea that singularities are to be avoided at all cost, just as callous and cruel people make great play with the word "sentimental." But the saints became saints largely owing to their courage—to the courage that enabled them to rise above the common or bourgeois level.

SAINTLY MOTIVATIONS FOR DIET

When we look clearly into the lives of the great saints, we discover that they were very singular indeed in all that relates to eating and drinking. Nor will it do to say that this singularity of theirs was dictated by purely penitential considerations.

They were bent upon becoming truly spiritual—and it would really seem as though truly spiritual people required careful feeding. Certainly many of the austerities of sanctity were inspired by motives of expiation. But asceticism, after all, aims always at doing for the human soul what gymnastics aims at doing for the human body. Its object is to produce an equilibrium or harmony between our lower and higher nature.

Asceticism aims at establishing some sort of peace between those aspects of the human person that are at variance with one another—between body and soul. It would subject body to soul not in the sense in which a slave is subjected to a master, but in the sense in which a pliable tool is subjected to the hand of a skillful workman. And if a tool is to be a pliable tool—a tool easy to work with—it requires very special treatment.

The saints were well aware that the body is the providential instrument of sanctification, the tool with which the soul must work. They knew, moreover, that the soul will never be able to get good work out of a body that is recklessly and thoughtlessly fed. The old notion that they simply despised their body must be revised. On the contrary, they had a very enlightened consideration for it.

The pagan philosopher Philo maintained that the

more immaterial we are, the more intelligent we become. He might have added, the more *spiritual,* although the word "intelligence" as used by him has a real spiritual significance. But the Christian writer Clement of Alexandria endorsed the dictum of Philo at the same time that he amplified it. "Wine and flesh," he said, "give strength to the body, but render the soul feeble and languid."

It is not the heaviness of the body that matters. St. Thomas had a very heavy body, yet he was a real mystic. Moreover, his day's work would have exhausted the energies of half a dozen men.

Gerard Groote had a body even heavier, yet he was a mystic and, moreover, he was the first practical mystic—that is to say, the first great contemplative who managed to combine apostolic labors with the repose of the cloister. It was thanks largely to sane management, to fasting and abstinence, that there was nothing gross or unwieldy about these heavy bodies—that they did not weigh their tenants down.

"Food," said St. Bonaventure, "ought to be a refreshment to the body and not a burden." On this point the saints were uniquely enlightened.

Charles de Foucauld, before his conversion, lived the usual life of a man of the world. He experienced all the usual discomforts that we somehow believe to be inseparably connected with the necessary business of nourishing the body. When later on he entered the abbey at La Trappe, he was astonished to find how refreshed and vigorous he felt under the Lenten fare. "Pleasant and comfortable" are the words that he used, and he added: "I have not felt hungry for a single day."

A SPECIAL DIET FOR SAINTS?

Is it being seriously suggested that there is a special diet for saints? It would seem so. In the beehive, the food for each class of bee is very carefully selected. The less refined forms of nourishment are forbidden to those destined to the more elevated and aristocratic functions.

The example of the beehive, of course, proves nothing. It is, however, an analogy, and it really is not easy to see how high spirituality could possibly thrive on the "customary" sort and quantity of food. The "usual sort of feeding" is an irrational feeding, and St. Thomas says that irrational feeding darkens the soul and renders it unfit for spiritual experiences.

The great contemplatives were practically one and all vegetarians, and fasting was their daily bread. This was because they knew by instinct what we know by experience: that excessive eating and a diet of animal products produce vibrations that make the body and mind unfit for the repose and tranquility essential to a life of meditation. Thanks to these nervous vibrations, we find it difficult even to support the burden of consciousness, and we have to be rushing to and fro using up the false and unwholesome energy that is generated in us.

It is undeniable that the modern man badly needs tranquilizing. He wants to rid himself of at least fifty per cent of what he calls his "intensity." He talks about keeping up his strength; and this strength that he keeps up by excessive and thoughtless eating and drinking commonly turns out to be a dangerous and unhealthy thing.

The fasting and abstinence of the saints purified

their bodies and therefore their minds and hearts. A field cleared of weeds is better able to yield the crops expected of it. In a similar way, their asceticism loosened and ventilated the soil of their soul and disposed it for the practice of contemplation.

St. Teresa was doubtless right when she said that no one can pray well whose body is in a tortured and irritable condition. This implies that the education of the body must be taken in hand with a view to the education of the soul. "Take even bread with moderation," wrote St. Bernard, "lest an overloaded stomach make you weary of prayer."

St. Jerome's rule that one ought to rise from a meal able to apply oneself to prayer and study is in reality a sound hygienic rule that the saints had the good sense to realize, and the strength of mind to be able to carry out. In the book of directions that he wrote for nuns, St. Alphonsus insists in the plainest possible terms that the success of their morning meditation will depend largely upon what they have eaten for supper the night before.

THE BODY-SOUL CONNECTION

The saints were probably better acquainted with the subtle connection between body and soul than has been supposed. Virtue, according to St. Augustine, is the art of living properly; and the saints were supreme adepts in this art of living properly. They understood its technique, and diet is part of that technique.

This reality is impressed upon us by the Church day after day during the season of Lent. "O God," she prays in the Preface of her Lenten Mass, "who by this bodily fast extinguishes our vices, elevates our understanding, bestows upon us virtue and its reward . . ."

Nature, of course, is the enemy. It is our fallen nature that pulls us down. But it may well be that we ourselves make nature heavier than she need be, as Blessed Henry Suso implies: "The setting of the sensual nature is the rising of the truth."

Certainly we have it in our power by reckless and irrational feeding to make nature far more *hostile* than she need be. "The stuffing of the stomach," said St. Jerome, "is the hotbed of lust." "I abstain from flesh," declared St. Bernard, "lest I should cherish the vices of the flesh"; and he adds: "A man becomes a beast by loving what beasts love."

St. Alphonsus wrote: "It is certain that excess in eating is the cause of almost all the diseases of the body. But its effects upon the soul are even more disastrous." "The devil," the religious solitaries were fond of saying, "is vanquished by temperance."

"An unruly horse and an unchaste body should have their feed cut down," said St. Hilarion. And in his *Moralia* St. Gregory the Great wrote: "It is impossible to engage in the spiritual conflict unless the appetite has first been subdued."

It amazes us to read of the fasts undertaken by the saints—undertaken and carried through apparently with ease. St. Paul of the Cross fasted daily except on Sundays and Feast Days. St. Catherine of Genoa kept her famous Lents and felt, as she admitted, "better, stronger and more active than ever."

Blessed Anthony Grassi, the Oratorian, used to say:

"Abstinence is the mother of health"; and again: A few "ounces of privation is an excellent recipe for any ailment." He was, of course, a pronounced vegetarian and lived to be eighty.

Indeed, it was the all-round sanity and moderation of their general diet that enabled the saints to fast. As a rule, those stand in greatest need of a fast who cannot endure the very idea of it. It is the body that has been overindulged that cries out and rebels against the slightest lessening or curtailment of eating.

"Continual moderation," says St. Francis de Sales, "is better than fits of abstinence interspersed with occasional excesses." He might have added that it is a continual moderation that makes abstinence possible and easy.

VEGETARIAN SAINTS

It is undeniable that the saints are nowadays attracting attention to themselves from all sorts of unexpected quarters. In particular, those enlightened men and women who are trying to do something to end the enormous scandal of the modern diet are turning their eyes toward these ascetics and mystics of ours and acclaiming their sanity and intelligence.

Vegetarians are taking their stand upon the example of the saints and, as a matter of fact, in this matter they are on very solid ground. They cite the flight from animal food that is so uniform a feature of the saints' lives. They are delighted to hear that Blessed Anne Catherine Emmerich lived not on beef broth but on cherry juice; and they point triumphantly to the undeniable fact that the instances of the miraculous multiplication of food that abound in the lives of the saints have to do with oil and wine and bread and grain, and so on.

How many of the mystics ate meat? The Bollandists, who have researched so carefully the lives of the saints, perhaps could tell us, and it would be a very instructive little item of information. It would be equally interesting to have a catalog of the vegetarian saints. It would certainly be a bulky one.

The list would begin with the prophets and holy men of the Old Law. The section devoted to the New Dispensation would commence with the first of its saints—John the Baptist. His diet consisted entirely of locusts and wild honey and, of course, the locusts referred to are not the insects but the herb.

The solitaries who peopled the desert in such large numbers in the early days of Christianity lived solely upon the products of the earth. Honey figures largely in their diet as it does in that of the great religious orders that flourished during the Middle Ages. Moreover, the primitive anchorites regarded it as very imperfect to eat cooked food.

These two apparently insignificant little facts have fairly made the modern-day food reformers sit up and take notice. St. Anthony the Hermit ate herbs, honey, and dates. When, after long years of fasting and abstinence, he emerged from his cave, the assembled monks were amazed to find, instead of an emaciated corpse, a fresh and vigorous, young-looking man.

The monks of St. Finnian's great monastery at Clonard in Ireland studied and plied their manual tasks on porridge alone, with a piece of dried fish added as a luxury two or three times a year. St. Paul of the Cross and his first companions lived in their retreat at Monte Argentario, Italy, on legumes and herbs, with fish on very rare occasions, and meat only three times a year.

The Curé of Ars is probably the only saint who ever tried to live on grass. He had to give it up in the end in favor of potatoes and lettuce with a little bread thrown in. The Curé found this simple diet very convenient indeed, and it served him in good stead for many a long year. To it he certainly owed much of his elasticity, his amazing energy, and his utter indifference to the petty circumstances of heat and cold and rain and dull weather that so easily throw us out of form.

St. Jordan of Saxony tells us of St. Dominic that "never did he even on his journeys eat meat or any dish cooked with meat, and he made his friars do the same." Even during the arduous task of preaching the Lent, St. Lewis Bertrand never ate any but vegetarian fare. People wondered where he got his energy from, and perhaps the said vegetarian fare could have told them.

St. Rose of Lima, from the time she was a young girl, lived on bread and the herbs she cultivated in her own garden plot. "We have bread, salt, butter, and potatoes," wrote St. Julie Billiart in one of her letters, "and we are the happiest women in Ghent." St. Cajetan confined himself to beans, vegetables, bread, and water, and sometimes a little wine.

TEMPERANCE, THE MOTHER OF HEALTH

Indeed it was thanks largely to their diet that so many of the Fathers of the Desert preserved a vigorous and uniform health and lived far beyond the ordinary term of existence. A great number of them were centenarians, and St. Arsenius actually reached one hundred and twenty years.

"Medical science" explains these astonishing facts, says Abbé Gaume. "It declares that temperance is the mother of health, prevents all those diseases that are the result of a weak digestion, renders external injuries less dangerous, soothes incurable evils, calms the passions, preserves the senses in their integrity, maintains the strength of the mind and the clearness of the memory."

It would be foolish, of course, to draw rash and general conclusions from this aspect of the saints' lives. But perhaps the day is approaching when in the interests of the higher spirituality the whole question of diet will have to be reexamined. It does seem as though the sane and hygienic tradition that the early Christians bequeathed to us has suffered some interruption.

Modern eating and drinking is not very Catholic after all, and it may be that in consequence, souls among us that might be on the wing are being driven down by the pressure of bad feeding. At any rate, food reform is not self-indulgence. It is the man who has no fads at all about food that is often a self-indulgent man. "I can eat anything," he says, and sure enough he sets about doing it.

A rational diet is a Catholic diet. The penitential discipline of the Church has a genuine hygienic foundation, as indeed the Church herself proclaims in her Lenten Office. According to this declaration she did not consider it beneath her dignity to have regard to bodily health when instituting Lent.

Certainly the spirit of Catholicism is more favorable to vegetarianism than otherwise, and it is clear from history that the ecclesiastical laws regarding fasting and abstinence were inspired to a great extent by cultural and civilizing considerations. Our Anglo-Saxon forefathers, for example, had to be weaned from their over-fondness for meat by drastic penalties. Altogether, Catholics ought to be in the very vanguard of the food reform movement, whose line of advance is, after all, in the direction of our Catholic tradition and the example of our saints.

THE IMPRESSION LEFT BY THE SAINTS

IF SECULAR history has been rather unjust to the saints, that unwritten yet authentic record which we call Tradition has more than made amends. The English historian John Richard Green lamented that his brethren had over-occupied themselves with wars and conquests and paid but little heed to the figures of the missionary, the poet, and the philosopher. He might have added "of the saint"; for certainly we shall look in vain in the usual sort of history for any mention of St. Francis of Assisi or St. Vincent de Paul.

Worse still, the insertions of some historians have been even more deplorable than their omissions. For example, Henry Hallam dismisses the most potent spiritual and social force of the Middle Ages in the following contemptuous terms: "Francis was a harmless enthusiast, pious and sincere but hardly of sane mind, a man who was much rather accessory to the intellectual than to the moral degradation of mankind."[108]

Fortunately, however, as St. Augustine once put it,

108 Henry Hallam, *History of Europe During the Middle Ages* (New York: Colonial Press, 1899), II, 197.

securus judicat orbis terrarum—"The judgment of the whole world is secure!" The average man is often a far better judge than the scholarly specialist who may pass his life in a dream of learning without ever having his sleep broken by a sense of the reality of things. The devotion of mankind is a more durable record than any printed book.

"What is the end of fame?" Byron asks; and he answers his own question: "'Tis but to fill a certain portion of uncertain paper."[109] But the fame of the saints depends not upon their paper panegyrics, but upon their good works. And if some of them were undervalued in their lifetime and misrepresented after their death, the general loyalty and enthusiasm of posterity have been a glorious act of reparation.

A PERMANENT PLACE IN OUR AFFECTIONS

Historians have sometimes been at great pains to perpetuate the names of those whom succeeding generations have been equally anxious to forget. But on the other hand, we find the people spontaneously and without any effort treasuring the memory of their true benefactors by awarding them a permanent place in the affections of their hearts. Thus the historian William Holden Hutton says of St. Thomas à Becket, whom secular historians have done so much to belittle: "He was incontestably the most popular English hero of the Middle Ages; and he was a hero because he was a saint."[110]

---

109 Byron, "Don Juan," Canto II, stanza 218.

110 William Holden Hutton, *Thomas Becket, Archbishop of Canterbury*

This fame is a real pledge of their intrinsic worth, a token of the splendor of Catholic sanctity. The Scripture says of them that their sound went forth into all the earth (see Ps 19:4), and surely the strength of the echo does tell us something about the loudness of the sound.

The American poet John Greenleaf Whittier relates that when he was a boy, President James Monroe once passed in the night through his native town. This flying visit of the President coincided with the visit of a travelling circus. Whittier did not see the great man, but in the morning, noticing in the fields the marks of the elephants' hoofs, he at once concluded that they must have been made by the President, since he felt that such gigantic footprints could only have been made by the biggest man in the country.

Even without being fanciful at all, we may fairly argue that the deep and lasting impressions left by the saints are real evidences of the greatness of the saints. It is quite impossible to belittle those who have carved out for themselves so lasting a niche in the temple of fame.

The heroes of this world did succeed in rousing multitudes to passionate enthusiasm. But for this, their presence was required. The very soil of France rose up at the approach of Napoleon Bonaparte, but when he finally departed from her coasts, the soil slipped quietly back again into its place.

Fame, says the cynical world, can survive everything except time, and the fame of the saints has stood this most difficult of all tests. They may have died unrecognized

---

(London: Sir Isaac Pitman & Sons, 1910), 2.

and unappreciated. But they died in the assurance of being blessed and venerated by a grateful posterity, and this is a form of glory as magnificent as it is rare.

The seventeenth-century king Charles II of England is said to have recovered some important papers he had lost by praying to the thirteenth-century saint Anthony of Padua. This trifling incident does throw some light upon the hold that the saint had upon the public imagination and esteem centuries after his death.

LASTING TRIBUTES

People have often wondered at the popularity in Scotland of the name Adam. This is a traditional and, by this time, probably an unconscious testimony to the memory of St. Adamnan, the biographer of Columba.

The Welsh people have accepted the leek as their national emblem, and this is their permanent tribute to St. David, from whom the suggestion came in the first instance.

The bird known as the stormy petrel is so called because, like St. Peter, it walks upon the sea. And sailors never care to have clergymen on board, because the shipwrecks associated with St. Paul's voyages have somehow never been quite eradicated from the seafaring mind.

The shooting stars that appear in August are called St. Lawrence's Tears, so that one saint at least has written his name upon the sky without any help from modern aviation.

These trifles all witness to the impression left by the saints.

The saints have impressed their personality upon

the very weather. We have "St. Martin's Summer" and "All Saints' Summer" and "St. Luke's Summer." There is a whole batch of "rain saints." St. Swithun of course holds the place of honor in England, but in Scotland the rain is or was associated with St. Martin; in Flanders and in Germany, with St. Godelieve; and in France, with St. Medard.

The latter in fact is known as "the Master of the Rain." The legend runs that he was journeying in company when a thunderstorm broke that soaked everyone to the skin except himself. He was protected by an eagle that spread its wings over his head like an umbrella. The French people say that if it rains on his feast, June 8, it will go on raining for forty days.

During May the French keep the festival of the three "ice saints"—Mamert, Tancrace, and Servais. The tradition is that if there is frost when their name-day falls, the frost will last for a week.

MARKS ON THE LANGUAGE

The cult of the saints has left marks upon the English language that nothing during the past four hundred years has been able to eradicate. We speak of a person being maudlin, that is to say, stupidly sentimental. The word is derived from St. Mary Magdalene, who was usually represented by the old painters with a lackadaisical face and with eyes swollen with weeping. The French, similarly, refer to a lachrymose person as a regular Madeleine.

Tawdry, meaning cheap and showy, is a corruption of St. Audrey or St. Etheldreda. At the annual fair held in her honor in the Isle of Ely, cheap and showy lace called St. Audrey's lace was sold. This gave rise to the word "tawdry" to describe anything gaudy or in poor taste.

Another interpretation, however, derives the word from the notorious disorder and litter which grew up about the saint's shrine at the season of the pilgrimage. But the first derivation can be relied upon. The English poet Edmund Spenser mentions tawdry lace in one of his poems; William Shakespeare refers to it in his *Winter's Tale,* and John Fletcher in his *Faithful Shepherdess.*

In Catholic days those who were forever dangling at the heels of others were said "to follow like a Tantony pig." This is said to be an allusion to the pig that figures in the life of St. Anthony the Hermit and acted as his attendant.

To be "drunk as Blaises" and to be told to "go to Blaises" is in each case a reference to St. Blaise. A certain amount of disorder was associated with the keeping of his feast, and this accounts for the first expression. The second is readily explained by the extraordinary faith that medieval England had in his intercession.

"By George," of course, speaks for itself, and so does "O Christopher." "Robbing Peter to pay Paul" refers to the chief Apostles, as a Latin couplet dating from the twelfth century shows.

In the ages of faith the saints were regarded as the great healers. To them were brought the sufferers whom the leeches and apothecaries could not cure. St. Genevieve was invoked for the burning sickness and for inflammation of the eyeball; St. Catherine of Alexandria for headaches; St. Bartholomew for convulsions; St. Firmin for cramp; St. Benedict for erysipelas and stones; St. Lupus for pains in the stomach; St. Hubert for madness; St. Appolonia for neuralgia and toothache.

Some of them ranked in popular estimation as real specialists, so much so that the particular diseases they cured were known by their names. The gout was called St. Maurus' evil; leprosy, Job's evil; cancer, St. Giles' evil; chorea, St. Guy's evil; common colds, St. Aventinus' evil; the bloody flux, St. Fiacre's evil; and so on.

SAINTS AND PLANTS

The association of certain specified plants or flowers with the saints is a notorious feature both of Catholic art and of Catholic devotion. In many cases the association is obvious. For example, the lily symbolizes the purity of a virgin; the palm, the victory of a martyr; the olive, peace of heart; and so on.

Sometimes, however, the connection is not apparent at all and must be sought either in some fact or legend or tradition identified with the saint in question.

St. Elizabeth of Hungary is commonly shown with a lapful of flowers. It is recorded in her life that when she was carrying food to the poor and her husband accosted her, the food was changed into a nosegay of flowers.

St. Thérèse, the "Little Flower," promised to let fall a shower of spiritual roses as soon as she had reached her reward. In this way the rose has become her emblem.

St. Thérèse, however, is not the first or only Carmelite to be associated with roses. St. Angelus is sometimes represented in art with a shower of roses falling from his mouth. This signifies not only the eloquence for which he was famed, but the eloquent zeal for purity that occasioned his martyrdom. Like St. John the Baptist he was put to death at the instigation of one whose immoralities he had publicly denounced.

Sts. Cecilia, Rose of Viterbo, and Rosalia of Palermo and others have roses for their emblems. St. John de Matha, the founder of the Trinitarians, has even contrived to get hold of a blue rose besides a red one. This is no doubt an indication of the red and blue cross that ornamented the habit of the Trinitarians.

One of the souvenirs of the Portiuncula chapel in Assisi is a leaf or leaves from the miraculous rosebushes of St. Francis that grow in the garden of the friary adjoining it. These rose leaves are stained with what look like spots of blood. The tradition is that the saint, when assaulted by temptation, threw himself into a thicket of briars and that, in consequence, the briars were changed into roses in full bloom whose leaves were stained with the saint's blood.

The flowering cross that is sometimes seen in the hands of St. Hugh of Grenoble symbolizes the fruitfulness of his terrible physical and mental sufferings. For forty years he was afflicted by illness and anxiety, and for some time before his death by loss of memory.

At least four saints have trees for their emblems. Pictures of St. Bavo show him kneeling beside the hollow tree in which he lived as a hermit. St. Zenobius is represented standing beside a tree that is bursting into leaf in order to indicate that he is the patron saint of the "flowery city," Florence.

St. Boniface, the Apostle of Germany, is depicted with his foot resting on a felled oak. His felling of an oak used for idolatrous purposes was the occasion of the conversion of a large number of pagans.

St. Bonaventure sometimes appears with a tree in the background, on which hangs his cardinal's hat. This scene of course recalls the story of how he received the news from Rome about being appointed to that office.

One of the emblems of St. John of God is a pomegranate surmounted by a cross. After his conversion he had a vision in which the Divine Child appeared holding a pomegranate in His hand and saying to him: "Go, you will bear the cross in Granada." (The pomegranate is called in Spanish *granada.*)

These few explanations serve to show the intelligent study of the life or legends of the saints that guided artists in their choice of symbols.

In many cases, of course, the identification is the outcome of the pious ingenuity of the faithful—a pious ingenuity that certainly testifies to a faith at once living and poetical. For example, the yellow flower known as the cowslip is sometimes called St. Peter's wort, Peter's key, or keys of heaven. (In Germany, it is *Schlüsselblume,* or "key flower.") The name comes doubtless from the resemblance that its blossoms bear to a bunch of keys.

So too the edible plant known as the samphire (a corruption of St. Pierre), is also called the *herba di San Pietro,* because it is usually found growing on the seashore. Again, it is said that the plant called herb robert derives its name from St. Robert of Molesmes, the founder of the Cistercians, because he used this plant for medicinal purposes.

The common (or wood) avens, which was considered an antidote to poison, is also known as the herb-bennet or St. Benedict's herb, owing to the saint's well-known victory over those who attempted to poison him.

The pig nut was popularly known as the St. Anthony's nut, because this famous Egyptian solitary was regarded as the patron of swineherds. In fact, it is said that to this day a farmer in County Kent will refer to a young pig as a "reg'lar little Ant'ny."

FEAST DAYS AND BLOSSOMS

Not infrequently this or that plant is associated with this or that saint simply because it happens to be in bloom at the time of the festival. For instance, there is the laurel of St. Lucian; the Christmas rose of St. Agnes; the whitlow grass of St. Vincent de Saragossa; the winter hellebore for the Conversion of St. Paul—because all these feasts occur in January. In February, there is the primrose for St. Agatha and the crocus for St. Valentine. In March, the early daffodil is assigned to St. Perpetua, and St. Benedict has a plant of his own, the herb bennet.

The harebell was assigned to St. George, according to the poet, because:

> On St. George's day, when blue is worn,
> The harebells the fields adorn.

At the end of the same month (April) the tulip was associated with St. Mark, and after him on May 1, the red tulip with St. Philip. Trinity Sunday has the herb trinity. The narcissus was reserved for the Triumph of the Holy Cross:

> Against the day of Holy Cross
> The crowfoot gilds the flowery grass.

St. John the Baptist has a plant of his own, St. John's wort, or wild rye. St. Peter has the yellow rattle, or yellow cockscombe. As it has been said: "The yellow cockscombe, which now flowers in our fields, is a sign of St. Peter's day, whereon it is always in flower to admonish us of the denial of Our Lord by the Prince of the Apostles."

Later we have St. James' cross or St. James' wort. The camomile is associated with St. Anne from the supposed derivation of its botanical name—*Matricaria*—from *Mater cara*—the dear Mother. The Michaelmas daisy is well known.

On October 1, St. Remigius has the St. Remy's lily. Holy Innocents' Day (December 28) has the "bloody heath." In England, the hawthorn was for some reason or other associated with St. Lawrence. Taverns were put under his protection, and because his image was commonly decorated with hawthorn blossoms, the names of some of them were corrupted into "Bosoms" Inn.

And what are we to think of the gigantic body of legend that grew up around the memory and personality of the saints—except that even this is of the highest value in illustrating the tenacity of the hold that both their memory and personality had upon the public imagination? It detracts not at all from the greatness and glory of these saints to say that many of the marvelous stories told about them are not true. Legend is the poetry of history, but it is much more: It is in a way a test of greatness, since only personages of outstanding character are ever able to inspire it.

SAINTS AND PLACE NAMES

It is impossible to make even a superficial study of geography without being confronted by the indelible traces of the inspiration of the saints. In a literal sense they have written their names upon the map of the world.

Europe was to some extent colonized and populated before Christianity came upon the scene. Many of the place names of our continent were, therefore, already determined, and naturally they have been retained. Nevertheless, the geographical vocabulary even of Europe is to an enormous extent Christian and Catholic and eloquent of the posthumous influence of God's servants.

Montalembert asserts that nearly three fourths of the towns and villages of France owe their origin to the monastic orders. That this is no exaggeration is proved by the names they bear to this day. Spread a detailed map of France upon the table and use a magnifying glass, and each circle of observation will be found to look like a miniature Litany of the Saints.

The district round Marseilles, for example, has never forgotten its association with St. Mary Magdalene and has erected monuments to her memory and to that of her relations in the shape of nearly a dozen place names. Brittany, of course, is unique, and in the neighborhood of Brest practically all the communes are named after saints.

What is true of France is, in a measure, true of her neighbors. The map of Spain, Italy, Portugal, Belgium, Switzerland, Austria, and Germany testifies to the deep and lasting impression that the heroes and heroines of Christian sanctity made upon posterity. Even Iceland, the last stronghold of European paganism to fall, bears witness to the zeal of the saints who labored for its conversion.

The straths of Scotland, the valleys of Wales, and the glens of Ireland speak to us still of the holy men and women who once inhabited them. Wales and Cornwall are altogether remarkable in this respect.

In the case of Wales, some knowledge of the Welsh language is necessary in order to appreciate the significance of the names that cover its countryside like a mantle. The "jaw breakers" such as Llangollen, Llangoven, Llanwyddelan, Llanbrothen, and so on, which confront us on its rail station platforms, are keeping alive the memory and name of St. Goan, St. Govan, St. Gwendolen and St. Brothen. Cornwall gives us among a host of lesser names St. Ives, St. Just, St. Agnes, St. Columb, St. Tudy, St. Gennis, St. Breward, St. Petrock.

SAINTS ON NEW WORLD MAPS

Turning to the map of the New World, we find that the saints have had practically everything to themselves. The New World was a Catholic discovery, and it was for the most part unchristened, so that Catholic piety was able to "let itself go" over the whole of that immense field. It certainly "let itself go" to some purpose. The oldest continually occupied city of European origins in what is now the United States is St. Augustine.

The great explorers and navigators who opened up the highways of the ocean and discovered the New World were Catholics. They not only carried the faith of the Old World with them, but they impressed it upon the territories they occupied. It is only necessary to go through the index of a really good atlas to realize how abundant and indelible these impressions are.

The entire continents of North and South America, through the mouth of their towns, rivers, mountains, provinces, bays, and capes, speak the language of the Catholic Church, and they do it more especially by means of a perpetual invocation of the saints. Columbus called his first halting place *San Salvador,* "Holy Savior." The first island that he reached on his second voyage he named *Dominica* ("belonging to the Lord"); *Trinidad* ("Trinity") indicates the termination of his third voyage; and so on.

Paraguay's "Mother of Cities" was called by the colonists *Asuncion* ("Assumption"). One of the earliest colonial districts in Brazil was *Espírito Santo* ("Holy Spirit"). Jacques Cartier named the St. Lawrence River; Pedro Álvarez Cabral called Brazil *Vera Cruz* ("True Cross"); Hernando Cortés also named his first colony in Mexico *Vera Cruz.*

Naturally the Incarnation was uppermost in their minds. In the Pacific there are three Christmas Islands. Ascension Town is in Bolivia, Ascension Bay in Mexico, and Epiphany in South Dakota. There is Jesus Island off Peru and *Corpus Christi* ("Body of Christ") in Texas.

It goes without saying that Our Blessed Lady is well represented. There is first of all the whole state of Maryland in the United States. The origin of the name appears from the letter written by the Jesuit Father Andrew White: "On the 25th of March (the Annunciation) we celebrated Mass for the first time. This had never been done in this part of the world before." This was in 1634.

In North and South America, St. Mary or *Santa*

Maria are found over sixty times; *Rosario* ("Rosary"), twenty-seven times; Virgin, sixteen times. There are in addition two sets of Virgin Islands, one in the Atlantic and the other in the West Indies. Assumption is found five times, and Conception or *Concepción* over thirty times. There is an island of *Madre de Dios* ("Mother of God") and a river of the same name in South America.

Coming to the saints, we can give only a short selection. The Apostles, first of all, are all well represented. St. John, or *San Juan,* is the favorite, and is found over one hundred times. St. Joseph appears thirty-seven times, and *San José* fifty times.

St. Michael or *San Miguel* is found over fifty times; St. Peter or *San Pedro,* seventy times; St. Paul or *Sao Paolo,* thirty-six times; St. James or *Santiago,* fifty times; St. Thomas, fifteen times; St. Louis or *San Luis,* eighty times; St. Nicholas, thirty times; St. Anne, forty times; St. Barbara, fourteen times; St. Rose or *Santa Rosa,* forty times, St. Patrick, three times; and St. Thecla, twice.

There is one St. Bridget in Kansas; and All Saints, or *Los Santos,* is found eight times. St. Mary Magdalene or *Magdalena* is found twenty times. Sts. Ambrose, Anselm, Andrew, Blaise, Bruno, Cajetan, Clement, and Casimir are all represented. St. George is found some fifty times; St. Francis, twenty times, *San Francisco* being his best example; and finally, St. Anthony is found in sixty places of the New World.

If you run your eye over the map of the territory surrounding the North and South Poles, you will see a very different spirit at work in the naming of the physical features of those areas. They bear little trace of a religious influence, and for the most part perpetuate the names of the explorers. This is, of course, useful, but it is in glaring contrast with the spirit of the ages of faith and of those who sought not their own glory, but the glory of Him whose Name they bore, whose message they carried, and whose saints they loved.

THE SAINTS OF THE MOUNTAIN TOP

OUR religion, being the religion of Our Lord, is Catholic. That is to say, it is intended for all-comers. It has none of that exclusiveness which imparts to certain modern forms of religion a look of propriety and primness—a superficial sort of superiority.

Let somebody found a sect and restrict membership to "enlightened" people, and the result will undoubtedly be a showy result. There will be nothing grubby about such a sect, and it will attract attention by the sheer respectability of its appearance and probably by its high-minded devotion to the cause of humanitarianism. It will concentrate all its attention upon one or two things, and therefore will do them remarkably well.

But the Catholic religion is not a sect at all. It does not pretend to be a collection of perfect people, a museum filled with prize specimens, an aristocracy of saintliness. There are well over a billion Catholics in the world, and the Church aims at doing something for all of them.

For some she can do but little. She can raise her children only as far as they wish to be raised. This means that among us there are various levels of spiritual life, various grades of spiritual development.

Too many, perhaps, never rise very high nor advance very far. All promise renunciation at baptism. But the majority, no doubt, will continue to reduce the renunciations of Christianity to a minimum, comforting themselves all the while with the thought that God is a Gentleman (whatever that may mean), and with the other thought that God is easily pleased—which at second thought does seem to cancel out the first.

SAINTS OF THE MOUNTAINTOP

On the other hand, our religion can and does guarantee to take us as far as we care to go and even much farther. If we aspire to the highest possible levels of perfection, it will be found always equal to our aspiration, and always far ahead of it. The Catholic ideal is seldom achieved, but it is never outstripped. Some, however, have come near to reaching it, and these we may christen the saints of the mountaintop.

Whether we call them mystics or contemplatives or ecstatics, they represent the supreme triumph of our religion, its most attractive advertisement. The entire catalogue of sanctity has nothing more splendid to show, nothing more utterly heavenly to offer, than these eagles of the spirit who, as St. Thomas says, enjoyed while still on earth a keener measure of the Beatific Vision than is actually granted to some of those who are already in paradise.

"It is normal and usual," says a modern writer, "that those in whom immense spiritual riches are stored should be hidden in the bowels of the earth." They are hidden, it is true, but not in the bowels of the earth. They do not appertain to the earth at all. We may, in fact, apply to them the words that the poet Percy Shelley used to depict the ethereal and almost preternatural character of the skylark.

> Higher still and higher,
> From the earth thou springest
> Like a cloud of fire;
> The blue deep thou wingest,
> And singing still dost soar, and soaring ever
> singest.[111]

To reach them is, of course, impossible. But in order to approach them, you have to journey far and to rise high. Their heads are among the stars, and their feet seem to rest upon the earth without touching it.

In very truth they have their "conversation . . . in heaven" (Phil 3:20, Douay-Rheims). For this reason, Blessed John Ruysbroeck, who is the prince of mystical science, was compared to an eagle whose home is on the loftiest peak and who is able to fix its gaze upon the sun without blinking.

Going even farther back to St. Denys the Areopagite—or rather to the great mystical writer of the fifth century called by that name—we are confronted by one who hardly appears to be made of flesh and blood. He has been called the first of the mystics. And he seems to have breathed a rarefied atmosphere and to have made a nest for himself on the very threshold of eternity, which he sees by means of vivid flashes of grace, while meantime

111 Percy Bysshe Shelley, "To a Skylark."

he remains calm and unruffled like a reporter jotting down his notes.

St. Lydwine made regular excursions into heaven and "picnicked" with her guardian angel on the fields of paradise. Similarly, the biographer of St. Passidea of Siena says of her that she spent more of her time in the other world than in this.

In fact, you cannot draw near to study those masterpieces of grace without feeling instinctively that you are quitting the realm of prose and entering that of pure poetry. For example, when St. Bernard tries to initiate us into the more intimate secrets of the inner life, "his prose," as Francis Thompson remarks, "rises into a beauty which is essentially that of penetratingly ethereal poetry." When he comes to describe the nuptials of the soul with God and "depicts in lines of light that bride who loves only for the sake of loving and being loved," his idiom ceases to be human and suggests the language that the angels use in heaven.[112]

Even those who have undertaken to write about these great mystics have been compelled to discard the phraseology of this workaday world of ours and to embellish their pages with the word pictures of symbolism. Thus, for example, St. Bonaventure describes St. Francis of Assisi in poetic language whose figures of speech all relate to the upper reaches of the firmament. He is the "Star of the Morning," the "Rainbow of Peace," the "Messenger of Christ" who lived the life of the angels, the "Second

---

112 Quoted in Everard Meynell, *The Life of Francis Thompson* (New York: Scribner's, 1914), 172.

Elijah" who was transported bodily to heaven.

Even the great English poet Richard Crashaw seems hardly to know where to get words with which to describe St. Teresa:

O thou undaunted daughter of desires!
By all thy dower of lights and fires;
By all the eagle in thee, all the dove;
By all thy lives and deaths of love; . . .
By all thy brim-fill'd bowls of fierce desire,
By thy last morning's draught of liquid fire;
By the full kingdom of that final kiss,
That seized thy parting soul, and seal'd thee His.[113]

WHAT IS MYSTICISM?

Mysticism is not easily defined, although many definitions have been given. We select this one from the seventeenth-century Dominican Thomas de Vallgornera: "Mysticism is the most perfect and exalted contemplation of God and the most sweet love of God intimately enjoyed and possessed."[114]

It is not so much a science as the living of a life. Some of the most eminent of the mystics have set forth its principles and theories in a most scientific manner, but they had to lead the life first of all. Mere study of textbooks will never produce a mystic, just as mere acquaintance with the science of prayer will never enable us to pray well.

---

113 Richard Crashaw, "Upon the Book and Picture of the Seraphical Saint Teresa."

114 See Thomas de Vallgornera, *Mystica Theologia Divi Thomae* (Turin, 1890).

St. Thomas Aquinas, St. Bonaventure, St. Denys the Areopagite, St. Bernard, St. Angela of Foligno, St. Catherine of Siena, St. Catherine of Genoa, St. Gertrude, St. John of the Cross, St. Teresa of Ávila, Blessed Henry Suso, Blessed John Ruysbroeck—these are the more notable saints who, themselves mystics, have told us in a masterly way what exactly it is all about.

Among them all, Blessed John Ruysbroeck, the Flemish contemplative, the Hermit of the Green Valley, probably deserves the place of honor. But opinions are fairly divided between him and St. John of the Cross. To the Latin races, the latter will no doubt make the stronger appeal. But there are certain qualities in Ruysbroeck that seem to stamp his piece of work with the mark of absolute supremacy among mystical treatises.

St. Teresa of Ávila, who came long after Ruysbroeck, has been described as "an admirable psychologist destined to sum up the rules of mysticism, to explain its workings, to take to pieces the various parts of its mechanism." Indeed, the science of mysticism owes its most orderly and lifelike classification to this woman, an extraordinary woman it is true, but still a woman.

Indeed, women figure triumphantly in the history of the higher spirituality, and in his Prologue to the *Visions and Instructions of Blessed Angela of Foligno,* Brother Arnold sees in this circumstance a providential lesson. He says:

> So that the wisdom of this world, which puffs up with arrogance, should be confounded, God has raised up a woman of the secular state: bound to the

> world; entangled by ties to husband and children and riches; simple in knowledge; weak in strength; but who, by the power of God infused into her through the cross of Jesus Christ, has broken the chains of the world and mounted up to the summit of evangelical perfection. This woman, in fact, has not only proved that it is possible to observe and to keep to the way that the tall giants of the world assert cannot be kept; she has also shown that it is an easy way and full of delight. O heavenly wisdom of gospel perfection! You have opposed to men a woman; to the proud, one who is humble; to the learned, one who is ignorant.[115]

This lesson is preached with even greater eloquence by the example of Blessed Anne Catherine Emmerich, who belongs to modern times. Born in 1774, the child of poor peasants, she had from infancy long conversations with Our Lady. She obtained from heaven permission to suffer for others and to relieve the sick by taking upon herself their maladies.

It was during the long martyrdom of her ailments that she had her wonderful visions. In these she was transported to Palestine and was allowed to follow the scenes of the Passion in all their detail. Vivid pictures of the sufferings of Our Lord unfolded themselves before her while she was bedridden and bleeding from the wounds of her stigmata.

---

115 See *The Book of the Visions and Instructions of Blessed Angela of Foligno: As Taken Down From Her Own Lips by Brother Arnold, of the Friars Minor* (London: Thomas Richardson and Son, 1871), "Prologue."

She mourned and wept, reduced to nothingness by love and pity for the torments of Christ. Although she was quite illiterate and had never read a book nor seen a painting, she has narrated what she saw in a prose style unique in its realism and having no relation to any known literature. She even describes in detail the surroundings of Jerusalem and the landscapes of Judea, although she had never visited the Holy Land.

Mystical literature does not make easy reading. Written for the initiated, it presupposes some experience of the inner life, the intimate dealings of God with the souls of those who devote themselves entirely to Him. But there is a class of literature that addresses itself to simple people, to ordinary Christians who are willing enough to fly but whose wings are not strong enough to carry them very high.

The Imitation of Christ is an excellent specimen of this diluted sort of mystical literature. Thomas à Kempis does not belong to the front line of contemplatives, but he was a real contemplative nevertheless, and his masterpiece was written for ordinary people living in the world who aspire to the spiritual life.

A KIND OF DISEMBODIMENT

"Let us die to ourselves," cried out St. Bonaventure; "let us impose silence on solicitude, on desire, on the phantoms of the senses. And in the train of the Crucified let us pass from the world to our Father." This would seem to suggest a kind of disembodiment; and such is actually what takes place and results in trances, ecstasies, elevations, bilocations.

It is related of St. Lydwine that in the end her body resembled a piece of glass that the spectator could almost see through. Indeed, the lives of some of these contemplatives became so supernaturalized that they were dispensed from the two most elementary laws of human nature, the necessity, namely, of eating and sleeping. St. Angela of Foligno, St. Catherine of Siena, St. Colomba of Rieti, Blessed Maria Bagnesi, St. Peter of Alcántara, and a host of lesser-known saints lived for longer or shorter periods on no other nourishment than the Holy Eucharist.

St. Lydwine of Schiedam was altogether unique in this respect. Not only was the Blessed Sacrament her only food, but she was physically incapable of swallowing anything else. It is related in the account of her life that a misguided and unscrupulous priest, wishing to test her sanctity, communicated her with a host that had never been consecrated. St. Lydwine received it from his hands but immediately rejected it.

The priest then pretended to be scandalized and accused the saint of profanation. "No," she said, "it is easy for me to distinguish between the Body of Christ and a simple wafer of unleavened bread. If this host had been consecrated, I should have swallowed it without the least difficulty. But I know that this one has not been, for my whole nature revolts against consuming it."

Among the number of those who contrived to live entirely or almost entirely without sleep we may note St. Catherine of Ricci, St. Colette, St. Christina, St. Elphide, and St. Agatha of the Cross.

PRACTICAL MYSTICS

As has been said, Gerard Groote is usually described as the first of the *practical* mystics, because he was a kind of pioneer of the art of combining the highest possible spirituality with a very active life of charity. This is not to suggest that contemplatives are unfit to play their part in worldly affairs. This is a prevalent notion, but it is an erroneous one, as the history of the saints shows.

All the great mystics have been energetic and influential, and their business capacity is specially marked in a large number of cases. St. Bernard was a born organizer. St. Teresa, in founding and ruling her convents, displayed a shrewdness and common sense that astonished her generation and confounded her many enemies.

Thomas of Celano assures us that although grace made St. Francis very simple, yet he was not so by nature—not by any means. We must never think of him merely as a dreamy poet who went about preaching to birds and shaking hands with wolves. He was so practical that he did what the clever world proclaims an impossible thing—he demonstrated that detachment is a virtue that will work.

It was not at all easy to impose upon St. Francis. He was more than a match for the cunning of the sultan who accused him of dishonoring the Cross by walking upon the carpet of which crosses formed part of the design. He very soon saw through the postulant who "did hardly pray at all and never did any work but did eat bravely."

"Go thy ways, brother fly," he said as he sent him about his business. St. Francis was quite expert in handling the technical side of the religious life, for which he drew up codes and canons with all the precision of a notary. As for St. Bernard, even Voltaire was compelled to acknowledge that no man ever succeeded so well in reconciling the turmoil of worldly affairs with the austerity and detachment of the cloister.

Those who cultivate this higher spirituality end by becoming completely taken up with God and the things of God. They become supernatural through and through. They simply live in Christ and He lives in them, with the result that the whole of their existence is directed heavenwards.

They eat and drink and sleep and do all to the honor and glory of God. Prayer with such eminent saints is not just something lying alongside their daily life as a guiding rope lies alongside the hands of the blind. Instead, it is something worked into the very stuff of their life as the yeast is worked into the dough.

This explains that routine of recollection characteristic of so many of the saints that seems to be irksome and onerous. They fell to praying as often as they heard the clock strike or the cock crow. Sunrise and sunset, snow, hail, rain, wind, and tempest made them lift up their hearts.

St. Teresa saluted the Risen Christ as often as she looked out of a window—and she was fond of looking out of windows. As she admitted, she loved a cell that had a good view.

St. Vincent de Paul recited the *Lavabo* each time he washed his hands—and he was fond of washing his hands, having, as he said, a fad for spotlessness.

St. Mary Magdalen of Pazzi could never look at a

flower without shedding tears of gratitude to God who had, as she felt, created it in order to give her pleasure.

The great medieval poet and mystic Blessed Jacopone da Todi has described in limpid verses how the Divine Love took possession of his five senses, so that in hearing, seeing, tasting, smelling, and touching, he found the image of his Creator.

It is related of St. Felix of Cantalice that when he heard the Roman seminarians sing or say a fervent *Deo Gratias,* he immediately fell into an ecstasy, wherever he chanced to be—even in the street. It is hardly surprising that this remarkable Capuchin lay brother was nicknamed "Brother Deo Gratias."

Father Martinez, "the Apostle of Peru," is said to have used the same words of aspiration six hundred times a day. And St. Cuthbert describes in this way the deathbed of Venerable Bede: "I can with truth declare that I never heard anyone return thanks so unceasingly to the living God."

What G. K. Chesterton has noted is so true: "The great painter boasted that he mixed all his colors with brains, and the great saint may be said to mix all his thoughts with thanks."[116]

None carried this spiritual ingenuity as far as Blessed Henry Suso. He is unique among ascetical writers in that he has revealed and bequeathed to us a formula of contemplation to be used while shaving. Speaking of himself in the third person, he says:

---

116 G. K. Chesterton, *St. Francis of Assisi*, in *The Collected Works of G. K. Chesterton*, II (San Francisco: Ignatius, 1986), 75.

As often as he shaved himself, he said to Our Lord: "Ah, sweet Lord, if my countenance and mouth were as rosy as the hue of all red roses, Your servant would keep them all for You, give them to no one else; and although You look only to the heart, nevertheless I offer You in this a love token in testimony that my heart turns to none but You."[117]

THE ECLIPSE OF THE EREMITICAL LIFE

Some cannot help but regret the passing of the eremitical life. Certainly civilization seems to have over-fostered the herd instinct and is suffering in consequence. "All mischief," said the French philosopher Jean de La Bruyère, "comes from our not being able to live alone: hence play, luxury, dissipation, wine, ignorance, calumny, envy, forgetfulness of one's self and of God."[118]

Even in this modern world of ours there must be many souls destined by God to complete isolation as was Charles de Foucauld, the Hermit of the Sahara. Here was a man of our own day for whom the silence of La Trappe was not sufficient. He yearned to plant himself like a solitary tree in the waste of that African desert under whose burning sky he had first been moved to review his misspent life and to plan its amendment.

His immediate superiors and the Holy See itself sanctioned and blessed his heroic design, and by so doing recognized that such aspirations are by no means impractical nor mere things of the past. Worldly wisdom

117 Suso, 179.

118 Quoted in John Morley, "Aphorisms," in *Studies in Literature* (London: Macmillan, 1897), 63, n. 1.

might have said that de Foucauld would have done better to have consecrated his talents and energies to the task of converting the Arabs by appearing in their midst as an active missionary. But it is just possible that worldly wisdom is at fault in overestimating the value of activity.

In his introduction to a book by a great monk of our own times, Bishop Hedley writes: "Perhaps the less a monk thinks about converting the world, and the more he thinks about converting himself, the more likely will it be that the world will be converted."[119]

Canon James O. Hannay said of the ancient monks that they aimed to be good rather than useful. He observes: "It is perhaps just because they denied themselves the satisfaction of aiming at usefulness that they were so greatly used."[120]

The slow and meager results of the strenuous efforts we make to convert non-Catholics may be due in part to our failure to realize that they are influenced far more by what we *are* than by what we do or say. De Foucauld's example may yet be found bearing practical fruit. None knew better than he the difficulty of converting the Muslim, and he always insisted that the thing would be done primarily by means of the exhibition of Christian heroism.

Failing the call to the solitary life, there are assuredly many whom God calls to the life of contemplation. It is the tragedy of far too many of these souls that, owing to

---

119 Bishop John Cuthbert Hedley, "Preface," in Rt. Rev. Abbot [Luigi] Tosti, *St. Benedict* (London: Kegan Paul, Trench, Trubner, 1896), xxiv.

120 James O. Hannay, *The Wisdom of the Desert* (London: Methuen, 1904), 21.

lack of encouragement or through positive misdirection, they are diverted from their true vocation and tactfully steered into one or other of the useful religious orders.

But of course we are living in an age of transition. Nearly all our traditions have been interrupted. Still we can well hope that with the return of normal conditions the spiritual life will be able to function with all its pristine exuberance.

It is false to say that the Church, spiritually, has passed her season of flowering—that she flowered so luxuriously in days gone by that the plant has exhausted itself. There is no decrepitude about the arm of God or about the works of God, and He can—and doubtless one day will—raise up out of the very stones descendants to those who made this once an island of heroic and contemplative saints.

THE REMEMBRANCE OF THE SAINTS

THE FURNITURE of the mind consists chiefly of memories. Someone once said with poignant truth: "Happy are we if among that furniture there are no pictures that have to be turned with their face to the wall."

"The wealth or poverty of our intellectual life depends mainly on the memory." Thus wrote the English educator Mother Janet Erskine Stuart. What a mysterious faculty it is to be sure, and what power it has to sadden or to gladden us, precisely because it is a receptacle that rejects nothing, a vessel that preserves the worthy and the unworthy alike.

To the memory we have recourse when all else in the cupboard fails. As a rule, it outlasts the other faculties, is left floating when the senses and reasoning powers have foundered. "Time robs us of all, even of memory," says Virgil; but indeed this seldom happens.

St. Alphonsus toward the end was threatened with the loss of his reason. "What will the world say," muttered the lay brother who watched by his side, "what will the world say if Monsignor Liguori should go out of his mind?"

But the old saint was listening as he dozed. "And what," he replied, "if it should be God's will that Monsignor Liguori should go out of his mind?"

St. Hugh of Lincoln is the patron of those who have lost their memories, but he never lost his own except partially. He forgot pretty well everything in the end except how to say his prayers, and he would repeat the Our Father three hundred times in one night.

Old people live in the past, and the saints were no exception to the rule. Our Lord is very good to the aged, perhaps because in His mortal body He never knew the infirmity of bodily decay. In the twilight of the desolate autumn of life, in the midst of the falling leaves, He allows a breath or two of the springtime and early morning of our existence to fan our withered cheeks, and on the fading horizon He lets us see the old familiar landmarks.

A history of the French revolution describes in this way the last hours of the unfortunate Georges Jacques Danton, one of the revolutionary leaders who fell out of favor with his comrades: "During the short period that elapsed before his execution Danton's mind, in a distracted state, reverted to the innocence of his early years. He spoke incessantly about trees and flowers and the country."[121]

In the lives of the Fathers of the Desert, we read that in his hundredth year the face of St. Anthony lit up and shone like the sun when he was reminded of the ardor of his first fervor. So, too, the deathbed of St. Damien de

---

121 Adolphe Thiers, *The History of the French Revolution, 1789 to 1800*, trans. Frederick Shoberl (Philadelphia: J. B. Lippincot, 1894), I, 377, quoting Sir Archibald Alison's history of the revolution.

Veuster was consoled by the recollection of what he had tried to do for God. "Fond memory brings the light of other days around me."[122]

Saints and sinners alike owe something to the fact that the memory is the only paradise from which man cannot be expelled. St. Augustine says in his *Confessions:* "I have never forgotten You, O Lord, since the hour I first learned of You. Ever since I learned to know You, You have remained in my memory, and I find You there whenever I call You to remembrance and delight myself in You."[123]

THE CULT OF SAINTS, A REMEMBRANCE

The cult of the saints is above all a remembrance. *Memoriam venerantes*, in the Canon of the Mass, says: "Honoring the memory in the first place of the Virgin Mary, as also of the blessed Apostles . . ."

In the early Church the one great privilege accorded to the recognized saints of each locality was an annual mention in its liturgy. This official cultus was, of course, at first confined to the martyrs. The earliest example of the public veneration of saints who were not martyrs dates from the sixth century, when a church was dedicated in Rome to Sts. Silvester and Martin.

This effort of the primitive Church was directed to keeping alive the recollection of what the saints had done and suffered. The "Acts of the Martyrs" were publicly

122 From the poem "The Light of Other Days" by the Irish poet Thomas Moore.

123 St. Augustine, *Confessions*, X, 24.

read in the assemblies of the faithful on the anniversaries of their death.

Indeed, the great aim of devotion to the saints is to detach our thoughts and hearts from this world so that to some extent we may, as St. Paul desired, have our "conversation . . . in heaven" (Phil 3:20, Douay-Rheims). The same St. Paul did not hesitate to call us the fellow citizens of the saints: *Vos estis cives sanctorum* (see Eph 2:19).

As members of the same human family, they are our kith and kin, of course. But also in a vivid and living way they are related to us, present with us, and solicitous for us. As Cardinal Henry Edward Manning wrote: "No trial can isolate us; no sorrow can cut us off from the communion of saints. Only a thin veil, it may be, floats between us and them."[124]

The gifts they lavished so freely upon the generations with whom they lived and worked are always at our disposal. We can draw upon them at any time and for any amount.

> Sunshine was he in the winter day;
> And in the midsummer, coolness and shade.[125]

How true these words were in the case of so many of the saints! Jordan of Saxony says of St. Dominic that "he appeared among his brother canons as a bright ray of sunshine . . . shedding around the fragrance of quickening

124 Cardinal Henry Edward Manning, *Sermons*, 2nd ed. (London: Pickering, 1850), IV, 312.

125 The words in which "an Arabian poet describes his hero," as quoted by Ralph Waldo Emerson in "Man, the Reformer," in *Works of Ralph Waldo Emerson* (London: George Routledge, 1883), 603.

life like the sweet scent of pinewoods in the heat of a summer's day."[126] One of the thousands who interviewed the Curé of Ars said afterwards: "I went in feeling cold and sour, and I came out feeling warm and sweet."

It is related of St. Anthony the Hermit that people went on pilgrimage into the desert just to get a look at his face. And St. Athanasius says of this same face that, unlike that of the sun, its splendor knew no settings. "The very sight of him made the beholder happy," has been written of yet another saint.

A BRIDGE BETWEEN THE HUMAN AND THE DIVINE

"You . . . must be perfect, as your heavenly Father is perfect," said Our Lord (Mt 5:48). But it is beyond the strength of mortals to imitate the Creator directly. So God has given us the sanctity of His saints, which like a bridge is flung across to span the gulf between the divine and the human and to make our passage easier. Holiness is the only attribute of God that we can imitate, so that in a very real sense, God's sanctity is seen in that of His servants. In fact, the saints are a revelation of God Himself.

In them He is seen not in the dark riddle of a similitude, but face to face, as it were. St. Francis of Assisi has been called the most Christ-like man who ever lived. The experience of Francis is a real approach to the experience of Christ. He copied the life of His Master as a pupil

126 Quoted by Hilary Carpenter, O.P., in "St. Dominic," in Frank J. Sheed, ed., *Saints Are Not Sad: Short Biographies of Joyful Saints* (repr., San Francisco: Ignatius, 2012), 196.

copies the teacher's writing example in an awkward and trembling hand.

"God made him like Himself in so far as it is given to man to be like God. Here is a Christian who was a man like you, unassuming in appearance, subject to your miseries, who can prove to you that your nature is capable of being molded to a divine model. He did not die on a cross, but he was granted the grace of bearing on his body the five seals of the crucifixion. Assisi is halfway on the journey to Jerusalem."

So, too, the prayer of St. Stephen, "Lord, do not hold this sin against them" (Acts 7:60) is an authentic echo of the cry that came from the cross: "Father, forgive them" (Lk 23:34).

What pleasant memories they have left behind! As soon as St. Maurus breathed his last, all the bells of the churches rang of their own accord. And when St. Anthony expired, the people of Padua ran through the streets shouting: "The saint is dead! The saint is dead!" Unlike so many of the heroes of this world, they are really worth remembering.

To some of them a special name, *myroblites,* has been given, from the Greek word *myron,* a sweet-smelling oil. After death, their bodies exhaled miraculous perfumes, the traces of which in some cases remained for years. Such, for example, are St. Agnes of Montepulciano, St. Mary Magdalen of Pazzi, St. Nicholas of Myra, St. Willibrord, and St. Rose of Viterbo. In a very real sense, however, the saints are all "myroblites," because their sweet savor, like that of Mary's ointment (see Jn 12:3), has gone forth and filled the household of the Church.

St. Francis has never been forgotten for a single day at Assisi, not even by the birds. They still fly into the marketplace when the Angelus rings as they did when he was alive. They come to be fed, feeling as sure of his protection today as when the sight of his grey habit encouraged them seven hundred years ago.

When Blessed John Henry Newman visited Milan soon after his conversion, he wrote to a friend as follows: "I am as much overcome with this place as I was at first. The greatness of St. Charles [Borromeo, Archbishop of Milan] is so striking. He is the very life of this place to this day. It is three centuries since he died, and yet he seems still to live. My mind has been full of him so that I have even dreamed of him."

In his life of St. Lydwine, Joris-Karl Huysmans, who visited Schiedam in order to collect materials, says of her: "She still lives at Schiedam, where the Catholics venerate her; and it must in justice be owned that the dissenters are not hostile to her. She possesses friends, too, at Haarlem, but farther afield her memory is effaced."[127]

Here is the tribute paid by a non-Catholic author to St. Clare, whose presence seems still to hover over Assisi:

> The peasants say that again and again she has been seen, and as I sit here in the light of the setting sun, looking at the horizon and the landscape which she knew, I feel somehow that I can almost believe it. Clare! Clare! The name sings itself softly in the silence of my heart. I hear it everywhere at last, not

127 J. K. Huysmans, *St. Lydwine of Schiedam*, trans. Agnes Hastings (London: Kegan Paul, Trench, Trubner, 1923), 237.

> only in my heart but in the chirping of the crickets and in the tinkling of the bells which in the distance swing from the necks of the flocks. . . . And now it seems that she herself is coming towards me and at any moment may appear round the bend of the distant road.

Of the manner in which the people of Siena keep the festival of their great saint, biographer Alice Curtayne says:

> So thoroughly is the city permeated with the presence of St. Catherine in this great commemoration every spring, that the children sing her hymn to themselves for weeks afterwards on their way to school, and their Latin is perfectly clear and confident. Climbing down the steep hillside to Fontebranda, one can hear boys of eight shrilling it to the high heavens:
>
> *Virgo decora et fulgida,*
> *Ornata Regis purpura:*
> *Electa, puro in corpore*
> *Christi referre imaginem.*[128]

Conditioned as we are, it seems necessary for us to reduce God in order to study Him in any sort of way—to diminish Him, if we may so speak, or rather to let Him reflect Himself by means of His servants as the sun does

---

128 Alice Curtayne, *Saint Catherine of Siena* (repr., Rockford, Ill.: TAN Books, 1980), 214. The Latin words can be translated: "O beautiful and resplendent Virgin, robed in royal purple, chosen to restore the Image, bearing the pure body of Christ" (translation by Dr. Kenneth Howell).

by means of the moon. This is an important aspect of the cult of the saints that has not escaped the notice of non-Catholics.

"To try and teach people how to live," wrote Froude, "without giving them examples in which our rules are illustrated, is like teaching them . . . to write verse by the laws of rhyme and meter, without song or poem in which rhyme and meter are exhibited. It is a principle which we have forgotten, and it is one which the old Catholics did not forget." They "detected, and were endeavoring to fill, a very serious blank . . . and one which, somehow, we must contrive to get filled if the education of character is ever to be more than a name with us."[129]

AN AGENCY OF MORAL REFORMATION

As a matter of fact, the remembrance of the saints has been a potent agency of moral reformation. Advice after all is rather like taxation: We do not care for too much of it, especially when it is direct. But example is a sort of indirect advice that appeals to the imitative faculty that is so strong in most people.

"What is to prevent me from doing what these have done?" St. Ignatius Loyola asked himself this question as he read the lives of the saints to beguile the monotony of his convalescence.

In the eighth book of his *Confessions,* St. Augustine describes the effect that the reading of the life of St. Anthony had upon his companions and later upon himself. They said to each other: "What are we aiming for?

129 Froude, *Lives*, II, 374.

For what do we serve the state? How long will it be before we rise to preferment? But if we desire to become the friends of God, we can do so immediately."[130]

St. Augustine himself cried out: "What ails us? The unlearned rise up and take heaven by violence, and we with all our learning, wallow in flesh and blood. Others are gone before us. Is it not a shame not to go after them?"[131]

When St. Athanasius read of the conflicts of the martyrs, he watered the book with his tears and prayed that he might be worthy to suffer the same for Christ.

St. John Colombini, who had been a wealthy magistrate of Siena, was led through reading the life of St. Mary of Egypt to leave the world and devote himself entirely to God and to the service of the sick.

St. Boniface, "the Apostle of Germany," fortified himself against the hour of his martyrdom by reading the acts of the martyrs.

St. Teresa of Ávila tells us how even when she was a child, her heart was inflamed with the love of virtue by reading the history of the Fathers of the Desert.

It was the sight of the Franciscan martyrs that drew St. Anthony of Padua to Assisi and St. Francis.

Henri, Duke of Joyeuse, Marshal of France, was led to change his irregular life by the accidental reading of the biography of St. Francis Borgia, which his servant left one evening on his table.

And in our own day we have this from the Little Flower:

---

130 See St. Augustine, *Confessions*, VIII, 6, 15.

131 See St. Augustine, *Confessions*, VIII, 8, 19.

> Yet I feel the call of more vocations still: I want to be a warrior, a priest, an apostle, a Doctor of the Church, a martyr—there is no heroic deed I do not wish to perform. I feel as daring as a crusader, ready to die for the Church upon the battlefield. . . .
>
> But to be a martyr is what I long for most of all. . . . I want to be . . . flayed alive like St. Bartholomew; thrown into boiling oil like St. John; ground by the teeth of wild beasts like St. Ignatius of Antioch, so that I might become bread worthy of God.
>
> Like St. Agnes and St. Cecilia, I want to offer my neck to the executioner's sword, and like Joan of Arc, murmur the name of Jesus at the burning stake.
>
> Open the Book of Life, my Jesus; see all the deeds recorded of the saints. All these I want to perform for You.[132]

If we do no more, we can at least recognize our own shortcomings in the virtues of the saints. This in itself will do us good. "It is," said St. Jerome, "a kind of candid and ingenuous confession to praise in others what is lacking to ourselves."

It is some compensation for our own coldness to know that God has been well treated and ardently loved by others. After all, His Son called us a flock, and as a flock He views us and balances the deficiencies of some by means of the generosity of others.

---

132 St. Thérèse of Lisieux, *The Story of a Soul: The Autobiography of the Little Flower*, Michael Day, trans. (repr., Charlotte, N.C.: TAN Books, 2010), 161–162.

Oh, though oft depressed and lowly,
All my fears are laid aside,
If I but remember only
Such as these have lived and died![133]

133 Henry Wadsworth Longfellow, "Footsteps of Angels."

TAN Books is the Publisher You Can Trust With Your Faith.

TAN Books was founded in 1967 to preserve the spiritual, intellectual, and liturgical traditions of the Catholic Church. At a critical moment in history TAN kept alive the great classics of the Faith and drew many to the Church. In 2008 TAN was acquired by Saint Benedict Press. Today TAN continues to teach and defend the Faith to a new generation of readers.

TAN publishes more than 600 booklets, Bibles, and books. Popular subject areas include theology and doctrine, prayer and the supernatural, history, biography, and the lives of the saints. TAN's line of educational and homeschooling resources is featured at TANHomeschool.com.

TAN publishes under several imprints, including TAN, Neumann Press, ACS Books, and the Confraternity of the Precious Blood. Sister imprints include Saint Benedict Press, Catholic Courses, and Catholic Scripture Study International.

CPSIA information can be obtained
at www.ICGtesting.com
Printed in the USA
LVOW08s2050210617
538886LV00004B/714/P